Voice Over Acting

Start a New Career in Audiobooks, Games, Podcasts, and more…

Voice Over Acting

Start a New Career in Audiobooks, Games, Podcasts, and more…

By Actor Academy

LIST OF CONTENTS:

Have you ever wanted to be a true "Voice Actor"? In other words, not just earning an income from recording promos, commercials and general announcer scripts as a voiceover, but actually learning how to boost your voice's flexibility to perform character voices and to act in various audio scenarios!

Wouldn't you like to be able to offer your voice, playing characters in animations, cartoons, and in the ever expanding video game industry?

We also will thoroughly train you in the narration and production of audio books, where you need to have a good voice acting skills for the character voices.

We hope you enjoy this course and will realise your true potential.

1 – INTRODUCTION – THE FOUR WORLDS OF VOICE ACTING

To be able to offer your services in every area of "voice acting" really is the icing on the cake for people who want to make a career using their voice, because if you have the flexibility to realistically "act" a variety of different types of voices, styles and characters, you really could "up your game" from straight voiceover narration, and be much more in demand for a wider scope of media projects.

We're so proud of this particular course, because it really does bring everything together. It's absolutely packed with so many solid gold tips and information from our many years of experience in the industry. We'll work with you to expand the basic skills of a voice over artist, so you'll be able to work on a much broader and often more lucrative canvas.

If you're a trained actor, and yet to get into the world of voice over work at all , don't worry, we have you covered as well in this course, and you may well take to voice acting itself like a duck to water. You may just need to learn the ins and outs of being a straight narrator, doing "announcer" voices, and to learn how to cleanly record audio in your own home studio, as well as how to edit your files, and you'll be off and running!

If you're a voice over already, and have taken one of our other courses, this one will certainly add more power to your elbow, and more flexibility as you will be able to add character voices to your arsenal, so you can audition for video game and animation work, as well as make audio books come alive. If you're a voice over that's done very little character work, we have some great tips for you, and also offer you our "character voice making machine!" You'll be able to adjust the many parameters and characteristics of your own voice to create a wide variety of different voices.

Basically, there are four different categories of work we're talking about here, the four "worlds" of voice acting. By the way, all the jobs we're talking about are FREELANCE ones, there aren't many "staff" voiceover jobs in the world today. There could be some staff continuity announcer positions at radio and TV stations, but no, we're all basically freelancers, which gives us the freedom to be in control of our own destinies! So, what are the four worlds of voice acting?

We have firstly the world of the "jobbing voice over", or sometimes called "voice artist" and as we've just mentioned, you may get given a few different character voices in scripts you're asked to record, and certainly you'll get a range of voice styles to read for various scripts like promos, commercials, training videos, award ceremony scripts and so on, but generally it's all your own voice.

THE FOUR WORLDS OF VOICEACTING
1- Mainstream voiceover
2- Audiobook production
3 - Animation voice acting
4- Game voice acting

Then the second world of voice acting is audiobook production, and this is a huge section of this particular course.

Why? Firstly, because it's a massively expanding world, and it's also quite easy to get into type of work for newcomers. It's a good place to try out your potential when it comes to performing character voices in fiction audiobooks.

With audio books, character voice performances are really a halfway-house between the narrator's normal voice and a full character voice. After all, people know it's YOU behind the microphone all the time, but when it comes to a character speaking in a fiction audiobook, you then have to give a decent nod to the personality and character of the voice at the time. But of course, recording audio book characters can be more challenging BECAUSE of this. Actors in a theatre or TV drama, can sometimes just play themselves, because other actors are there to play the other characters around them. In an audio book, you're actually doing everything!

The third area of voice work is animations, or cartoons if you like. Usually these are 2D or 3D animated films, usually aimed at children or young people, and the voices here certainly aren't usually your normal voices, and you need to perform a voice that is totally in character, and usually stereotypes are welcomed. For example, for years, Peter's been the character of Albert for Run Fox's children's app aimed at teaching non-English children the English language.

And finally, The Holy Grail of the voice actors' world, is getting work in video games, the industry that is actually bigger than the movie industry these days. Games sales seem to go up and up all the time and there are loads of new titles, many of them need actors. Good actors who can give stunningly realistic performances that can relate to the player.

Voice acting for the top-selling games is true, believable character acting as if you were on a theatre stage or movie, usually to a very high standard. But there are plenty of games companies where they welcome voice actors who can do solid stereotype type acting work, and who don't mind self-recording often long, very long scripts off an Excel sheet where you have to record huge variations of the same sort of thing, depending on what the other characters or the game player asks you!

4	SMission0019_Line1_Tuk_Companions	Humans and Eldun make for stran
5	SMission0019_Line4_Tuk_FearNot	Fear not, noble steward. I have a
6	SMission0019_Line6_Tuk_IDidNot	I...did not know that.
7	SMission0017_Line5_Tuk_NeverCook	I've heard much about the Eldun ı
8	SMission0017_Line7_Tuk_FearFire	The Eldun fear fire, do they not?
9	SMission0017_Line9_Tuk_Worship	We are humbled by the power of
10	SMission0016_Line12_Tuk_Back	Back, foul creatures!
11	SMission0016_Line14_Tuk_HailFriends	Hail, friends! It warms the embers
12	SMission0016_Line16_Tuk_Infested	Dark mana has infested our belov
13	SMission0016_Line20_Tuk_Steward	...A Lumen steward? Remarkable!
14	SMission0016_Line21_Tuk_PleaseFriends	Please, friends, I beg you. Accomp
15	SMission0018_Line5_Tuk_Merchants	I recognize those wagons! Humar
16	SMission0018_Line8_Tuk_HumansOnce	Those creatures were humans, or
17	SMission0018_Line9_Tuk_SoAbsolutely	I...I've never seen Dark Mana corı

When you come to do those sort of things you need to just try and imagine where you are and why you are saying these lines, to give you context which is very important. Remember, you are actually in that scene, you ARE that character, and you are not faking it. The lines are not just lines, you need to make the delivery REAL. Imagine a backstory to your character if you are not given one.

For this work, quite often, trained stage actors find playing characters in radio plays or video games and so on very easy, after all, it's the same work they do on stage or in front of the camera, but without any of the visual elements; although some actors DO also perform the visual side of performance by wearing Motion Capture suits and act the lines while doing the movements that eventually end up as animated characters on screen. This is the so call MOCAP technique, so if you ever see ads for "MOCAP auditions", you'll know what these are for!

Another job that voice actors could be asked to do is for dubbing. This is where you are normally in a professional dubbing studio, where they loop the same lines again and again in your headphones while you try to match the mouth movements of the actor you see on screen. This is usually needed when non English films are dubbed into English, and it's a great skill to get this right, but with a professional dubbing studio and a good translator who not just translates the sense of each line, but also the mouth movements correctly, it can be very satisfying, especially when your voice comes out of another actor's body on screen!

So existing trained actors may find voice acting for character work easy, but may find difficulties in performing straight "voiceover" narration, barking out hard sell radio or TV adverts, understanding the skills to correctly emphasis or to showcase words, or to fit scripts into exact times - skills that trained voiceovers find easy. On the other hand, many successful voiceovers just can't get into proper voice acting, because they either are not flexible enough with their different voice styles or accents, or their characters don't develop beyond stereotype, in other words, they just can't "act". Don't worry though, not everybody can ever be good at everything, and the point of this course really is for you to identify what you're really good at, and also what you could be even better at. That way, you'll see all the different types of jobs and styles of voices that are needed across the four main industries of the voice world, and we'll get you up to speed fast.

So we really hope you enjoy this course, let your inhibitions fly away, and you could be developing a whole variety of different personalities by the end of it, and boosting your career as a Voice Actor!

2 - WHAT EXACTLY IS A VOICE ACTOR?

So what's the difference between a "voice over" and a "voice ACTOR"? It's the extra flexibility that your voice can bring to the game. Nobody is ever going to be absolutely perfect at everything, but generally, a voice actor is someone who can easily move between the four worlds we described before, and tackle projects to a pretty good standard. It's someone who can do a great straight documentary narration one job, and then turn into a variety of crazy characters for an animation, and then do a couple of hours working on an audio book. That's what we're talking about here.

Of course, voiceovers or "voiceover artists" get scripts that need to be read in a variety of different styles, but it's still really your own voice. You could be asked to read in a corporate manner, a friendly and casual style, or in a "hard sell" style for commercials. And sometimes you may be asked to do some character voices. In the world of the voice actor though, you should be flexible enough not just to be offered bread and butter voice over work, for corporate scripts, promos, documentary narration, commercials and so on, but to understand how to shape your voice to be able to offer character voices.

The next section will offer you a very powerful tool that you'll be able to use to create a huge variety of different types of voices, styles, and character voices. But for the rest of this section, we're going to go through the first world, that of the "voice over", in a bit more detail, for people who are completely new to the industry. Now if you are a voice over already, and are just interested in doing more character work, and to get into audio books, games, and animation work, you're welcome to skip the rest of this and go on to the next section.

So if you'd like to read on… let's cover the world of the voice over. We do have other courses that will cover this in much more detail, taking you through every aspect of finding work, recording, editing, and marketing yourself, but here are the basics first of all.

A voice over artist is generally a freelancer, and they may either be someone with an agent, who generates work for them and calls them up when there is a job, or they may be completely independent, without an exclusive agent, and then they market themselves, and do the work themselves and invoice direct, without having to pay an agent.

Both types of voice over artist would be encouraged to have a studio at home, because even if you have an exclusive agent who finds all the work for you, quite often, clients want to hear a custom audition for every job, and that has to be recorded somewhere. Do you really want to spend the time and money hiring an external studio, just for an audition that you may not get? That's why it's important to set up a home recording facility, even just a basic one at home. In a later chapter, we go into this in great detail, as to what equipment you need, and where you can set up your recording facility at home.

YOUR POTENTIAL CLIENTS:
advertising agencies
creative digital agencies
animation houses
games companies
TV and radio stations
telephone marketing companies
audiobook production houses
translation agencies
individual freelance producers

So, what types of jobs are you likely to get? If you are someone with an exclusive agent, you will probably end up getting far higher paying jobs then someone without an agent, however the number of jobs may be far fewer. That's because most agents need to earn a living as well, so they're not going to bother chasing up the little $50 or $100 jobs, when they could be working on getting the $5,000 TV commercial jobs for you. Whereas if you are type of voice over like we are, independent, with various non-exclusive agents round the world looking out for work for us, then you are likely to have much more jobs, and be busier, but the actual jobs would be probably be lower paid. But that's no problem, because rather than hanging around waiting for the phone to ring from your agent, you're busy every day on a variety of jobs, and the little jobs add up. I personally don't mind chasing my own work and doing my own invoicing. If you'd prefer someone else to do that for you, and you are happy to pay that person, then go down the route of having an exclusive agent, which means every job that you get even people who contact you direct has to go through your agent.

The types of jobs that you can get as a voice over are extremely varied, and we wrote down recently about 50 separate types of jobs that you could get, which include all sorts of things, and not just the normal corporate video narrations, or training videos, or TV and radio commercials, voice overs are needed for all sorts of things, like phone announcements, award ceremonies, lift announcements and even reversing truck warnings! And don't think that the world is saturated with voice overs at the moment, because there's always room for people who are good all-rounders, and are willing to learn to improve their skills. Media is being created in massive amounts everyday around the world, and the amount is going up all the time. Since the pandemic started, and conferences got cancelled, how do you think that all information that WAS going to be imparted at all those conferences is getting across to people? The amount of corporate communications by recorded means, has absolutely rocketed, and it's going to get more and more important to have recorded information, recorded by someone who knows how to narrate, and record, to a high standard.

Some people have said that voice over work would decline with the advent of artificial intelligence, and the improvement in computer voices, and maybe on YouTube you've heard "FAITH – the First A.I. that can cry". This is impressive, but it's strange that the music is mixed quite high, probably to hide the artefacts on this artificial voice, and I wonder how long it took to actually get them to do it.

I'm sure that A.I. voices may well take over our voice work in areas like automated announcements on telephone, and maybe even some low budget training programs, but the true depth, breath, and emotions of a real human voice are very hard to replicate by a computer program. And why go to all that effort when you can simply communicate to a human what you need in a few seconds that would take hours or days to program on a computer? In particular, emotions are very hard for a computer voice to emulate, and that's why this particular course that focuses a lot on character voices, and emotional acting, will be even more important as time goes on.

The Voiceover gets sent the script(s) from the client along with details of the voice style , voice age, speed and duration, accent, etc....

So what are the practicalities of voice over work? Usually, scripts get sent to you after someone likes your show-reels on your website. Show-reels are examples of different styles of voice, you could have one file showing a corporate style, a casual style, or some simple character voices. So the client would send a script and say "I liked the voice style that you had on your third show-reel", or whatever. They may also give you information like "we need the whole script done in 90 seconds", or they may send you a video that has a rough voice over on. And you'll be able to see the pictures, hear the music in the background, and get an idea of the feel of the voice over style the end client is looking for.

Now why "end client "? Well, basically the end client, is the person paying for the whole thing. They own the company who are putting the training program out, who are paying for the advertising campaign, and so one. They may have hired an advertising agency, and that agency has hired a production company, or an animation studio, and then they find a voice agent or use a voice directory website, like Voics.com or Voice123 or even Fiverr, and you are at the end of this long chain, the voice over. So in a way, you have the hardest job, because you have got to satisfy everyone up the chain all the way to the end client. Of course, if the end client – who's paying for everyone along the chain - loves your voice to begin with, then everyone beneath them will also love your voice too!

Once you're sent the script and the information, you are normally left to get on with it yourself, to record and to edit, and to send back the master files. We've got more details about how to do this in another course about the software program Adobe Audition, but we do feature audio editing when we discuss audio books later on.

You're not always left alone to record though. Sometimes, and this happens on the high value prestigious jobs, you will be directed. This means either you go to a physical studio, or more likely, you will need to put your headphones on, so the clients comments can't be picked up by the microphone, and be directed through the session. This can be particularly stressful, if there are more than a couple of people directing you. We've been through sessions where five or even six people have all been putting their own direction in, and quite often give conflicting advice as to how they want you to record the next take! Anyway, after one of these sessions, you normally don't have to edit anything, which is the plus sides of a directed session. Normally you are directed via Zoom or Skype, or one of the more professional communication systems, and then you'd simply send the whole of your recording to the production company for editing, and you send in the invoice.

So I hope you found this basic overview of the world of the voice over interesting if you're a newcomer, and as I say, we cover much more of setting up your own voice over business, and more on the technical side in other courses. So see you in the next section, when will introduce you to your vocal control panel, which will be your secret weapon in being able to secure lots of interesting , fun, and hopefully lucrative voice acting work!

3- CREATING CHARACTER VOICES – YOUR VOCAL CONTROL PANEL

So, we have learned that the voice actor can easily tackle jobs in the four main worlds of: voice over, audio books, animations, and game work. A key part of this flexibility is the ability to create a wide variety of different voices, and characters. So this section will give you essential tools, to create a sort of imaginary control panel and give you all the parameters and changes you'll need to give you the flexibility to make a great variety of character voices.

Now, every one of us have got our own base voice, which you would usually use as a "narrator" type voice for animations, video game intros and promos, and of course audiobooks. You can if you want, create a complete character voice and use it for the narrator, but considering the amount of words that you would have to read across the whole audio book, it would be a very big strain on you and it would be difficult to keep the voice consistent as well. But you are welcome to try if you want to!

The voice that I talk on my videos is my normal "base voice". I don't put on any of the different extra parameters or filters we're about to discuss now. So what parameters CAN you change? What's on the "control panel" of your voice? In fact that's a good way to think about your voice, and how to adjust your voice for various characters.

Just imagine your voice has 10 separate controls that you can turn up and down and select different things. You've got inherent personality, accent, you've got the shape of your mouth and vocal apparatus to play with, you've got register, nasality, overall physicality, there is emotion , power of the voice, the speed or pace of speaking, and a "clip control" which determines whether the voice is clipped or legato and smooth.

These changeable parameters are the ones that I have developed over the years for all the audio book characters that I've recorded, and you're welcome to use this and adapt it and add to it for your own needs. And it's helped me enormously because you just need to work out what setting each control is on, and you've got a character voice. Unfortunately, unlike electronic equipment where you can store settings as a pre-set, the human brain has to remember the voice and also refer to a sample recording, like I showed you, so that you can slip into each voice again next time the character comes up in the book. Let me go through each of those ten "controls" in turn.

PERSONALITY

If I gave you a list of types of personalities, probably, I bet in your mind a type of voice would already pop into your head. A rather stuffy pompous person may speak a little bit like this, or a wide-eyed enthusiastic person may speak with great clarity and be very fast paced, and maybe jittery or nervous. So think about the personality of your character, and that's a good place to start for the voice that you could assign to them. What has the author told you about this character? How do they relate to the people around them?

ACCENT

So how many accents can you do? Sometimes you need to perform an unusual accent that you're only going to need for one project, and there are courses on accent tuition or even quick YouTube videos that can offer a useful guide to getting started to sound fairly authentic for the basics. So for German, for example, you'd learn that "W's" need to sound like the letter v, and "the" becomes "ze" and so on. But if it's an accent that you really just can't get to grips with, don't beat yourself up too much, the author has chosen you for your narration skills, and not for your skills in performing accents perfectly. As long as the book is enjoyable to listen to, and as long as the words are clear to hear, a nod towards the accent will be fine.

SHAPE

The shape of your mouth and your vocal apparatus can totally change the voice style. Try speaking dragging the top lip down. Now try to overcompensate to get the clarity out. Now, push the front of your mouth out as if it was a long snout. Maybe a character could have that type of voice, but of course, watch losing the clarity, and you wouldn't use a voice like this for a long time as it's tiring to listen to. Or try stretching your mouth very wide as if you were trying to say the letter E all the time, the shape of a post box. Try speaking like that all the time and there again a different voice emanates from your mouth.

Another type of change you can make to your voice is by simply expanding your throat inside. Just yawn for me now - and just feel what's going on inside your neck area. And just keep it in a sort of half-yawn, and now speak. It sounds sort of mellow, and this could be a nice touch to add to a character who has a rather posh, affected voice, to make it sound different from someone else. If they have an awful lot of words to read, I wouldn't suggest doing this, because it does hurt to keep this semi-yawn for any amount of time.

And don't forget that all these different shapes can then be mixed with whatever you selected on the accent control and the other controls that we've giving you here. So experiment, record yourself, and playback, but don't forget that clarity is key. And if you find it hard to get into that character and to stay there, only use those sort of voices, for minor characters.

REGISTER

Have you heard of the registers of the voice? The "Lar-in-geal Mechanisms" to give them the technical name. Different physiological adjustments of larynx enable the wide range of frequencies of the human voice; it's all very clever. This is the way we can adjust the vocal tract to give all the huge variations of vocal qualities and timbres of our speaking and singing voices. The vocal folds are named from zero to three (M0, M1, M2 and M3), each associated with lower to higher tones. Each of these membranes, the vocal folds, have differing lengths and thickness.

Classification of Registers Depending on the Laryngeal Mechanisms Involved			
Mechanism M0	Mechanism M1	Mechanism M2	Mechanism M3
Fry	Modal	Falsetto	Whistle
Pulse	Normal	Head	Flageolet
Strohbass	Chest	Loft	Flute
Voix de	Heavy	Light	Sifflet
Contrebasse	Thick	Thin	
	Voix mixte	Voix mixte	
	Mixed	Mixed	
	Voce finta		
	Head		
	operatic (M)		

M0 creates a low and nasty, creaky "vocal fry" sound. It's your human "sub-woofer" speaker in a way, no power, but it adds depth to the overall voice. Just use this M0 vocal fold on its own, and you'll soon get a sore throat.

Most speech for men and women is using the M1 and M2 folds. The upper end of that and into M3 gets into falsetto territory. Really skilled vocalists are switching on and off these 4 layers, whether they know they're actually doing it or not. That's the weird thing about creating voices. A doctor can say what's technically going on down there, but for us voice actors, we need to use psychological techniques to switch on and off the vocal fold layers to get the voice we want or need. For many actors, after lots of experimentation, they get the voice and then use a trigger word or catch phrase to get back into that voice, or think of an actual person, or look at a picture. Impersonators often use this technique.

NASALITY

As well as working on the basic vibrations of the vocal folds, you could also add in nasality, by lowering or raising the soft palate. If you don't know what that is, we do go into a lot of details in our Deeper and more Resonant Voice Course, but simply hold your nose and say AAH. Nothing happens. Now hold your nose and go "HANGGGGG". Wow! That's a difference! You're sending the air up the nose that you're now blocking. You're moving your soft palate, which is really the back door to the nose, up and down. Keep the soft palate down and you get a nasal sound, usually not wanted in rich voiceover work, but could be great for a character voice, especially mixed with an accent!.

PHYSICALITY

At voice over master class, we keep on going on how important physicality is when you're recording voice overs. Just by moving your arms around and emphasizing certain words and pulling yourself back and standing in a certain way and moving closer and further away from the microphone can totally change your voice, and really assist you in getting through difficult scripts.

So with characters, try moving around in a jaunty way, or move your head at a strange angle and try speaking like that. Or pretend that you're in pain while you're speaking…..squeeze yourself in….. Honestly it's amazing how many different types of character voices can come along when you just experiment. Just have fun, and record some voices and see what happens. Remember nobody can see you in the voice booth, so if any kind of physicality helps you to achieve and to sustain a voice character, then just do it!

EMOTION

So, at that point in the audiobook story, or video game, or cartoon, is it obvious the character is really upset, or angry, or wants to persuade the other character to do something? The sort of emotion you choose for each character at each part in the book really comes with understanding where you are in the story and for each character you really have to get into their shoes. How would they be affected by what's going on around them? Why would they speak in this way? Nailing down the right emotion at the right time will really make your characters sound much more authentic.

POWER

The power of voice includes volume and also can be wrapped up with emotion as we've mentioned before, and you may have some people who speak very very softly, and expect to be heard, or they could be softly speaking to themselves, almost like a mumble. And you may get an author who asked you to mumble some lines, but try and keep in mind the poor listener who does have to make out the words that you are saying, because they don't have the text in front of them! If you are in the voice booth and about to do some really loud lines, such as shouting at the top of your voice, remember to check back the loud section as soon as you've done it, in case you have over modulated, and have distorted the recording. Maybe you would like to experiment with recording the loud lines with the input to your computer or recording device at a slightly lower setting.

SPEED

Some people speak very fast and enthusiastically, and that's fine, but again, remember to keep the clarity in the speech! And some people speak ridiculously slowly. Now speed is very useful to you if you have two or three characters who all have the same accent, which is different from your main narrator accent, and it's a way that, if you can only do one type of foreign accent, you can differentiate the characters from each other. One person could speak faster or slower than the other one.

CLIP

The clip control on our vocal bunks, determines how legato the voice is. Some people speak in a much joined up manner, sounding like treacle or rich honey emanating from their mouths enjoying the resonance of each word flow into the next. Whereas other people have a much clipped voice, where the beginnings and ends are completely separate, and you could almost hear the slight pauses between each one, and certainly between the beginnings and ends of sentences.

Well, have fun experimenting with your new 10 control vocal control panel. Don't forget that if you learn a new skill on one of the categories, for example you learn how to do a new accent, suddenly you can add that to any of the other parameters so your amount of available characters goes up.

We're often asked about "other sex" voices when it comes to characters. If you're a man, of course you don't need to impersonate a woman's generally higher voice, or you'll end up in comedy Monty Python land. Simply take the resonance out, sound softer, raise the tone slightly and that will be fine for a man voice actor representing a woman character voice. The other way round, as well as lowering the pitch, women can sound manly by adding a bit of gruff or a pinch of a regional accent...you need to experiment! But don't worry too much about this. If you're a male narrator in an audiobook, and say "Barbara looked her friend and said..." or whatever, the listener is expecting to hear a female speaking anyway, so their brain will compensate!

4 - VIDEO GAME AND ANIMATION VOICE WORK

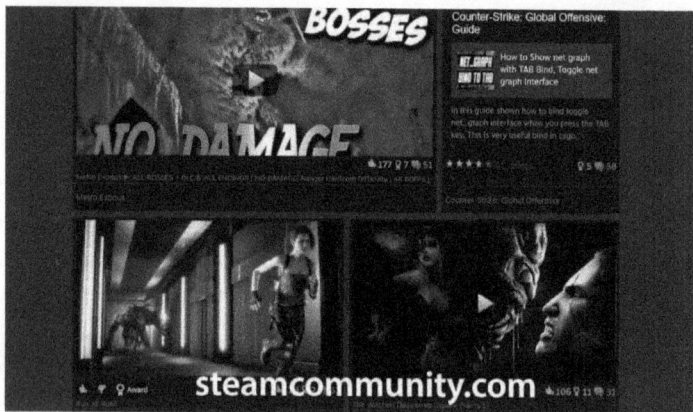

et's look at game voice acting. The big, international game companies behind the likes of Ghost of Tsushima, Call of Duty, The Last of Us, Mortal Kombat and so on, have huge budgets, and plenty of resources and time to audition voice actors to play the parts. They will extremely rarely book a voice actor off a show reel and send you the script to just "get on with it", unless it's a very small part. The world of the major video game is as big if not bigger than the global movie industry. They will usually hire via specialized agents and not contact voice actors direct, and the job will usually mean strict direction in the studio, usually in Los Angeles, line-by-line by experienced directors who really know their stuff. Recording usually takes days or weeks of intense work to get things right.

Now some video game companies don't mind the stereotype character type of voice, and both of us have had work recording character voices that the clients have been wildly happy with, and if you'd like this kind of work, it's usually the small to medium sized indie game company who work on this type of project with a theme that's usually humorous, or based on an existing historical or out of copyright work like Sherlock Holmes, The Roman Empire, a "steam" type game or something like that. In fact the Steam Community site, and also Kickstarter is a good way to find small indie games that are in development and they may not have been cast yet for voice actors.

Here are some of the scripts that I've been sent that normally come on an Excel spreadsheet. If you thought Excel spreadsheets was for accounts work, well no, the world of gaming has found their very useful for putting individual lines on and assigning them a filename. Most of the time, you won't have to worry about cutting up each line into individual files, thank goodness! Some of the game companies I work for, ask me to do 3 different takes of each line, and then they select their favorite take, or if they don't like any of them, that's when the retakes come.

	1	2
52	Squadplay Commands	
53	your squad under fire	CommandSquad_Un
54	squadmate down	CommandSquad_Sq
55	your squad has beed wiped	CommandSquad_W
56	squad vehicle ready	CommandSquad_Ve
57	Gameplay commands	
58	incoming strike	CommandGame_Inc
59	battle strike ready	CommandGame_Str
60	commencing strike	CommandGame_Co
61	This is air support incoming strike	CommandGame_Inc
62	This is air support battle strike ready	CommandGame_Str
63	This is air support commencing strike	CommandGame_Co
64	This is armor support incoming strike	CommandGame_Inc
65	This is armor support battle strike ready	CommandGame_Str
66	This is armor support commencing strike	CommandGame_Co
67	This is artillery incoming strike	CommandGame_Inc
68	This is artillery battle strike ready	CommandGame_Str
69	This is artillery commencing strike	CommandGame_Co
70	armored reinforcements, on the way	CommandGame_Arr

They could have asked to direct me over the headphones so they get the perfect take, but for a big game, when there are many characters doing things in the game, it's usually more efficient to do things this way. So you try and give three completely different types of interpretations, because you're never totally clear as to who you are relating to, or what circumstances you are in

What are the technical differences in recording drama material as a voice ACTOR as against general narration and voiceover work? In voice acting, you're usually allowed to ad-lib and make the scripts your own, unlike voiceover scripts where every word has been checked and approved and you can't change anything apart from to correct English grammar! You can add link words, leave longer pauses than normal, and you don't need to worry about breathing! For usual voiceover work, of course, you need to cut out or reduce distracting big breaths, but in voice acting, the breathing is part of the overall character personality! You can also move around the microphone in the voice booth to use the distance characteristics of the mike, as if you were moving around the room....unlike staying in one position like in standard voiceover. Just make sure you don't hit the microphone or the stand! You can leave dramatic pauses in voice acting too; this is very rarely allowed in commercial reads!

Once you are assigned a character, believability is everything. If you play video games, you'll know that the relationship between the player and the characters is very important, so you have to really "get into the character". For characters with more than just a few lines to read, if you're not given the following information, you need to ask the client, and they'll be happy to give it to you.

You need to ask for a picture of your character; even if the production company haven't created any animation of your character yet, they'll at least have a mock-up or 3 D still. This is very important as a visual anchor for your voice style or accent. It will help to remember how your character looks every time you need to "click" into that voice.

Physical description: British but with a bit of a pirate accent.
In his 50s. A skilled physician.
Personality: Wise, weak, overly protective.
Goal: Assemble the crew, and find his long lost friend, Mason Owen (
Jane's Father).
Realtionship to Player: Ally
Realtionship to NPCs: Ally to Mason Ovens, Crew Members.
Enemy to Fake Doc, Captain Ashworth.
Accent: British with pirate accent

Most of the time, because of confidentially, you won't be given the full arcs of storyline, but you CAN reasonably ask for where your character fits in to the plot and their relationship to other characters. Knowing this can make all the difference between saying the line "Why did you do that?" like this if they're an old pal who has just knocked over your pint of beer in the bar, or "Why did you DO that?" if the other character you're addressing has just massacred your entire family. So, understanding WHY you're saying lines and in what context is very important!

In the next section, we look at what you should and shouldn't put on your show reels, and one of the tips we gave you is don't put all your funny voices on one compilation reel and we'll explain why later, but one thing you can do to really up your game, and to improve your repertoire of different character voices, is just keep on doing different voices in the day. For example, let's say you have just been in a shop, and the shop assistant had a very unusual voice, or particular accent. Try and listen to every new nuance of that assistant's voice, then as you walk out the shop down the road, try and do it, probably under your breath if there are other people around you! But try and copy other people's little idiosyncrasies and voice patterns, and you never know what you can come up with. You may even come up with new categories to the voice character control panel we discussed earlier!

(Peter writing this) I was once on a long car journey on my own, and I was feeling a bit tired and fed up to be honest, but I thought I would practice my comedy laughs to cheer myself up, I wondered how many types of laughs I could do. So I went through the usual Halloween type eerie laughs, to some Santa laughs to some manic crazy laughs, down to some non-descript titters and guffaws. It certainly perked up my boring drive, and I learned a lot about what knew laughs I could perform. So please try doing things like that, particularly when you are on your own, not just in a car, but maybe on a long walk in the countryside. Just make up stuff, have fun! Even if the auditions haven't asked for it yet, imagine what type of voice you would do if you were asked to be a wizard, a witch, a troll, a demon, a unicorn, or all sorts of strange fantasy creatures you may like to imagine.

The other thing to remember about voice acting, is that it's not just words that you have to act, sometimes it's just non vocal performances such as grunting and groans and particularly in fighting games, sounds where you are wounded winded or dying, which is always interesting. You may also be asked to do strange alien voices or animal noises like the kind the voice actor Bradley Baker has recorded over the years for countless Hollywood movies and TV shows.

When you are doing these sort of things, you really can't be too self-conscious, it's sometimes very lucky that people can't see you in the voice booth groaning and dying. On the technical front, by the way, you're much more likely to peak too loud and distort the signal, or pop the microphone, or even hit the microphone when you fall back and collapse. So just keep that in mind when you're doing your non vocal performances!

So how do you get into voice acting work? For animations and games you need to get on the personal casting databases of specialized voice casting agents. Casting directors will work either for developers, the so called "devs", or the studios that produce the games themselves. Maybe they work through one of the outsourcing companies like Pit Stop, Liquid Violet, Sound Cuts, and Side and so on.

Studios and production companies that specialise in game recording:
Pit Stop
Liquid Violet
Sound Cuts
Side
Sounding Sweet
Liquid Crimson
SNK Studios

There's nothing wrong at all with creating a series of audio show reels with the voices and accents you can do authentically to demonstrate your flexibility, but be aware that a casting director for video games don't want to just hear a load of "voices", even if you want to show off your range of accents. For example, if they wanted a really authentic German accent for an English language game, they'd hire a German actor, wouldn't they?

More than just voices and nice accents, they need to hear realistic ACTING ability in your show reels, with you interacting with other voice actors. In fact, if you're clever, you could also BE the other characters in your show reels! These show reels would get you through the door of agents if you haven't got one already, or on to the database of recording studios and production companies who specialize in video game audio recording. We have more on this in the next section on auditions and show reels.

If you're an established voiceover already with your own studio and maybe you're subscribed to various so called "Pay to Play" sites like Voices.com or Voice 123, you won't find that many big voice acting roles for games on there. The ones that DO advertise for auditions tend to be small indie games that need some narration, a game promo or simple stereotype characters, but work is work and you may be perfectly happy with doing that.

We've put together some links in the downloadable resource of this course, but things change all the time, and I would suggest you enroll on websites such as Mandy.com, both the actors and the voice over sections of it, also Backstage.com has some really good leads sometimes. But simply Goggling "animation voice casting directors", or "game casting directors" will help you identify who are the main players in the game, and then try and seek these people out on social media. In fact, there are many game production companies who look out for talented voice actors by posting things on Twitter and so on, so follow these companies....you need to do a bit of detective work in the area you particularly want to get into.

5 - CREATING SHOWREELS AND
AUDITIONING

A s a professional "jobbing" voice over, the first of our categories we mentioned earlier, creating audio show reels is absolutely essential so that the end client can select the right sort of voice for their scripts. You would have a decent website as well, with all your show reels on, for easy download, so production companies can play them to their end clients.

You would create a show reel for a documentary style of voice, a corporate style, maybe a training video style, a chatty and conversational voice style, an "every person" type of voice as if you were a member of the public interviewed in the street, and maybe some deep voice movie trailer scripts if that is something in your repertoire.

Now, things get a bit more complicated when you want to get into voice acting work, where people are trying to cast characters, particularly for high end video games. This is because you are not likely to have a wide variety of different show reels that will cover the specific character that the video game producer has got in mind. But show reels are still important.

They will get you through the door of voice acting agents, who would see your potential, an agent who would specialize in getting work for their clients in video games, and animation work, and from then on, it would be the agent's job to persuade the producer or casting director of each specific game or animation project to ask you to audition. This may be a live audition in a studio somewhere, a down-the-line session, or maybe you will just get a part of the script sent to you along with some information about the character, and the context of the audition script, and you get asked to record a custom audition to send in.

When you do get the opportunity to do a custom audition, make sure you read absolutely everything that is given to you, because it will all be there to help you understand a whole load of important things: The genre of game, the target audience, the character you are, the characters you are playing against, the context of the scene you've been given, and therefore why you are saying what you're saying. Don't just look at your lines and have a brief glance at the character notes, say to yourself "oh, it's one of those types of characters" and then start to record your audition.

Look at the lines in the script before and after yours, because they're given to you, to give you context for your own lines in your audition, and you can then give it your best shot. Another thing you can do for an audition is to adlib a little bit, say a few words in character before the actual words of your audition script. This is called "pre-life"- it's putting something in character before the actual audition lines - something before the dialogue to help you get into it. Your pre-life may be something as simple as a little laugh, or even a long sigh, a noise of frustration or something, but as long as it's in character, the casting director who hears this in your audition will know that you thought a little more about it than just reading the words on the script. Ad-libbing a little bit before the actual audition, also will add an element of surprise when the casting director hears it after listening to possibly many others from other voice actors. You'll be remembered more for this, so you get a double whammy plus doing this, but only if it's appropriate with the audition script you've been given...

For high end video games in particular, you need to show you can act. You need to show the range of human experiences and emotional states and energies, and not just that you can do a reasonable Scandinavian accent, for example, or you can impersonate a celebrity, or do generally silly voices or whatever. As we've said before, if they want an authentic Norwegian accent, they would find a Norwegian person who can speak English wouldn't they? Accents are fine for audiobooks as we'll find out later. But for this genre, think acting. Could you play the part of a man or woman who has just discovered their partner is having an affair; or who just been fired; or who has just been wounded by a terrorist, or has just done their first parachute drop? You get the idea. Understanding a character's backstory so you know how to deliver their lines is so very important for this type of work.

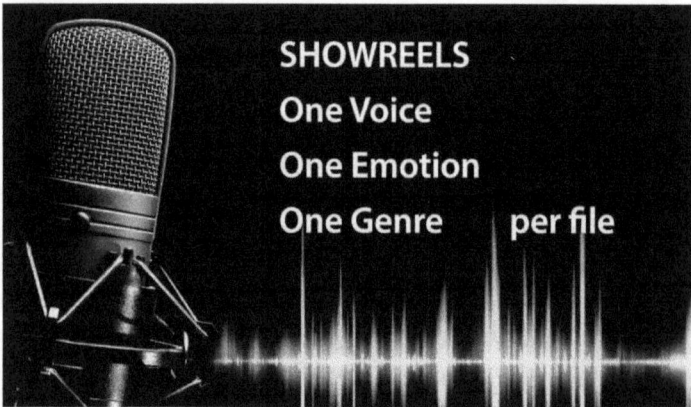

SHOWREELS
One Voice
One Emotion
One Genre   per file

We suggest that you don't waste your time creating show reels that are full of lots of different things all mixed together. If an agent is open to new people on their books, and you need to ask them before you apply as a courtesy, then you can ask them what types of show reels or examples you may send them, but usually a mixture of lots of different accents and voices is not what is really needed, as it won't really impress many people.

However, where this kind of show reel COULD BE useful, is for cartoons and animation work, where maybe in a project, characters have been developed, sketches have been drawn, and their characters have been worked out, but nobody has really thought of the voice for any of these cartoon characters yet.

So maybe you could be lucky and your show reel could be listened to and one of your voices could be a match in the mind of the producer. But you really need to create targeted show reels with one voice, one emotion, and one genre per file.

A mixed show reel is only good to initially interest an agent or a production company who will then invite you to audition specifically for a specific character for a specific project. Don't think that by creating a mixture of funny voices, on a compilation show reel, and then sending it out to everybody, will get you work, because it probably won't I'm afraid.

So what WILL impress an agent, to take you on, is if you can prove you can act in a natural and totally realistic and believable manner. If you already play video games, you'll know how important it is to be totally immersed in the gameplay. You may already be familiar with the work of top voice actors in the game world, like Troy Baker (no relation to Peter!) or Nolan North, who have made massive careers in the world of video games.

Listen to their work, and other voice actors you admire, maybe listen to Mark Hamill's explanation of his voice acting work on YouTube, and others, and in a way, get angry with these people, or at least jealous! If you think you could do their job, or if you think you could be even better than them with their voices, then this will give you an extra impetus in getting into the world of voice acting. By the way, if you are not into playing games, you can go onto YouTube and type in the games you're interested in hearing the flavor of, or type in "Let's Play" and you also put in the search bar "play through, no commentary", and then you'll be able to hear the actor's voices cleanly. This will give you an idea of the kind of acting work that's out there in different styles and genres.

If you haven't been lucky enough to have professional acting training, one cost effective way that you could move forward in creating realistic acting show-reels, and clips of performances that are totally believable and realistic, and also apply for auditions that you are offered, is to get a "Voice Buddy".

An ideal Voice Buddy is someone who is doing the same sort of thing as you, and someone that you will really trust and value their feedback. You would comment creatively and constructively on their recordings, they would give you that much needed objective perspective, and they would do the same with you. This system can work very well, especially if you aren't rivals, for example, if one is a young person and the other buddy is an older person, or you have a male and a female as buddies. The Voice Buddy system can work very well, and you may find someone via social media, and you don't even have to physically meet with the Internet these days do you?

Just share files and comment on each other's auditions and show reels, and be really critical as to what you hear. You may be able to assist your voice buddy in various tips such as not over rehearsing something before they record.

Some people new to acting, seem more natural, when they read an audition script first time, because somehow they put the little hesitancies and imperfections in, that you would get in natural speech and conversation with an unread script. Sometimes things that are over rehearsed, don't just sound realistic. So tips like that, that you can impart to your buddy can be really valuable if they are relevant.

You can maybe both learn acting techniques together, such as the Meisner Technique, where you get in touch with your emotions and you can perform realistically by using your imagination and by taking away self-consciousness.

You'd ask yourself, rather than making up an emotion and "acting" a scene, you ask yourself what would be happening in my life for me to say the lines this way? There is a whole world of acting techniques out there, so if you're a voiceover who haven't explored this area of acting before, see what's out there that's relevant to your experience and to the field of work you want to get into.

6 - USING A GAME DEMO PRODUCER

In the last section we talked about the advantages of using a Voice Buddy, which is a very cost effective, and often fun way of working with someone else where you can both assist each other. But if you have some cash to invest, we suggest that you also seek out a professional coach, a mentor or demo producer who deals in the kind of work you want to get into, and ask them to get great performances out of you. You'd ask them to put together your voice acting show reels, and specific audition recordings for big jobs. Many demo producers who have been experienced in the voice acting industry for years, may well have insights into specific jobs available at the moment anyway, and could even accelerate your career, but of course there are no guarantees. Google "game demo producers" or "voice actor demo production" "animation demo production" or "voice actor show reel production".

It's always important to get a mentor that you trust, and even well-known experienced voice actors, would not even think of putting together their own show reels and demos, because they value someone else's contribution to this whole process. Just be very careful before you take on any demo or show reel producer though, because some of them charge a lot of money, and so you need to be sure that you are going to get good value for your investment. Obviously checkout their reviews from other people first.

When you're choosing a demo producer, find out if they have got the actual skills you need for your own needs. Maybe you want someone who will give you pre-written suitable scripts or will direct you, but you're perfectly okay at your end on the technical side of recording auditions and editing. Maybe you need someone who is more on the technical side of recording or editing, so find out exactly the skills of the demo producers who are available.

The sort of information they would want to hear from you, is what of characters do you relate to? Are you a natural leader, or a follower, a goody, or a baddie? Are you naturally a strong character or a weak character? Where do you want to improve your technique in voice acting?

Here are a few technical practicalities with show reels and auditions. Casting directors want to hear what you really sound like, naturally, first of all. So at least always start off saying your name in your normal voice. Why is this? Well it's true, that the title of your audio file will have your name anyway won't it, or it should do! The reason is that casting directors want to know the voice that you are most at home in, your natural voice, because what's the point of casting someone who was putting on another character voice and then having to sustain that voice for the duration of the project, when they may have a perfectly good natural voice to begin with?

So, say your name at the start, this is normally called a "slate". For some auditions that you are asked to send in or upload maybe you are asked NOT to slate, or you need to just mention your agency, so always read audition instructions very carefully.

Something you may want to think about carefully particularly if you are auditioning for cartoon or animation work, is not to give a photograph of yourself. Your name will probably give away your sex, but some animation character voices sound so bizarre and different from anybody's photo, and that's fine! People cast with their ears and not with their eyes remember!

So maybe leave your photograph off your initial audition application for a cartoon job, particularly if it's a voice job vastly different from your normal voice. I wonder if Nancy Cartwright put her photo on the application when she auditioned to do Bart Simpson's voice.

By the way, if you are British, and you are applying to an American organization, don't be ashamed of your British accent, because it's an accent in demand around the world and particularly in North America; so don't think you need to American-ize your voice, although if you can offer a decent and consistent Mid-Atlantic or "international" accent, that's always a bonus. When I say British accent, I don't mean necessarily a "BBC" type or "R.P." accent, or Received Pronunciation.

If you have got for example a natural North East UK accent, or a Scottish accent, or one from the West Country, and that's your realistic natural base voice, then casting directors would want to hear that. Even if they don't particularly want to cast that accent now, they would be even more impressive when they hear the same person creating all sorts of other character voices, when your base voice is something completely different.

If the audition doesn't give very much information as to the type of performance that's needed, then take things into your own hands. This gives you an opportunity to show how flexible you can be. If one particular part of a script for the audition could be interpreted in two completely different ways, because you don't know the context of the particular dialogue, then record things in two completely separate ways. Put two takes on the audition file. But make sure they ARE completely different.

Don't waste someone's time with two very similar sounding auditions. For example, an interpretation could be in an "upset" type of emotion and the other one could be in a generally "angry" stance for example.

When you've recorded an audition and you have got the job awarded to you, go back to the original audition and listen to it very carefully. Try and work out what it was about that particular audition that captured the casting director's ear, and they may tell you more feedback anyway in the reply to you, with a request to perform "just like your audition" – BUT a little more this or a little less that.

If it is a mid to low value job, maybe they won't be bothered to direct you over headphones for the actual session, so it's even more important for you to listen to the audition that won you the job, so that you create that same voice, and send back files that are exactly what the client wants.

Good   luck   with   your   auditions!

7 - AUDIOBOOK NARRATION & CHARACTER VOICE WORK

If you're just getting into understanding character voices, or even starting voice over work itself, recording audio books is a good way to start. You might like doing just factual or non-fiction books which is fine - they are basically enormously long documentary type scripts, although there may be some character quotes in some factual books; but where your character work will really come alive will be in FICTION books, where quite often, there are different characters interacting with each other. Because the listener cannot see the text of the book or the script in front of them, you have to make it very clear as to who is talking to who.

Narration only fee PFH (Per Finished Hour):

$75 - $150

Narration + Editing & Production PFH:

$150 - $350

AUDIO
BOOK

In the following sections, we'll give you a load of tips for narrating audio books, as well as technical production techniques. Why is this important? Well, if you hire a studio, or studio hires you as "just a narrator", you really won't have much cash to take home at the end of the day for an audiobook. The average fee "per finished hour" to just narrate an average "non-name" audio book can be not great – just $75 to $150 per finished hour. But if you learn the skills we'll teach you to actually edit together the files after recording, in other words "produce" the audiobook as well, you can ask for $150 to $350 per finished hour, especially if you have a decent and fair author and/or publisher. The work is more satisfying as well if you don't just narrate it, but edit it and master it as well. This is called "audiobook production" and so basically clients would hire you as a narrator and a producer together. People with these joint skills are much more valuable in the world of the audio book, and if you are a narrator AND producer, you could either get contacted direct from authors or publishers, or you can work on one of the many audiobook platforms we'll discuss later.

Everybody loves a good read - either fiction or non-fiction (or factual), and we'll be covering both types of audiobook. Thanks to advancing technologies over the years, more of us have been able to enjoy hearing books read by the author or by a professional narrator.

Not only is it convenient to hear a book being narrated when you are on a long journey, having a walk or lying in bed, but also many people find the actual task of reading difficult due to dyslexia-type issues or visual impairment, so audiobooks are a literary lifeline for them.

Now, maybe you're a narrator or existing voice-over artist who wants to learn about audiobook production, or an experienced audio producer who would like to learn to narrate as well, or maybe you're an author wanting to know what's involved in narrating and editing together your own audiobook - or at least to be informed about the process if you are looking to outsource all this to someone else. We'll do our best to keep everyone satisfied.

We'll look at the skills and attributes of a good audio book narrator and look in detail at how you get paid, and the arrangements that narrators and authors have with each other and how you all get paid. Then there's a big section about preparing for recording, looking at adapting the manuscript that works well in a physical paper book or Kindle device, but maybe not so well for audio.

NARRATOR

AUDIO PRODUCER

AUTHOR / PUBLISHER

You'll learn how to keep consistent with your delivery and with character voices, how to multi task effectively, and to monitor the accuracy of what you're recording, and also keeping fatigue at bay as well as all the technical tips you need to know to make sure that your files will be accepted after the recording of course.

After recording, it's time for editing which will go into in detail, and we'll also let you know what to do with the revision notes from the author, which means re-recording sentences or sections and making sure they fit in with what you originally created. And then we'll talk about mastering and exporting so they get accepted by the main platforms that deal with audio books, as well as explaining how you can get work as a narrator and producer in audio books. If you haven't got your own recording facility yet, we'll cover that in a section at the end. And for authors and publishers who are using this course to expand their knowledge about the whole process, there's plenty of information for you too, including the distribution networks available for the finished audio book.

8 - THE AUDIOBOOK INDUSTRY

The world of audiobooks is greatly expanding, and that's something not many industries can boast of at the moment! In fact, the Audio Publishers Association of America have reported for the 8th year in a row, double-digit revenue growth. This year, audiobook sales just in the United States brought in 1.2 billion dollars, and that's up 16% in sales this year. The great thing is that there's still plenty of room for expansion in the audiobook market because it's still a small part of the total book sales, but audiobooks are actually getting more and more important in people's lives these days.

We've all got more stress and hassle than ever these days, particularly dealing with the pandemic, concerns with income, and so on, and enjoying an audiobook is a sort of oasis, a secret place and special world where people can escape to.

Yes, an audiobook is such a great medium to enjoy when you're out for a walk, in a gym, on a long journey in a car, or travelling on a train, it helps people absorb a story or a factual book that they are interested in, to escape the crazy world for a while with their ear buds or headphones on.

In general, people are loving audio experiences more these days anyway, as there is less time to sit down to consume television; radio listening is going up and so is listening to podcasts which is another huge growth area.

(Peter Baker writing this) I've been a voiceover and narrator over 40 years. My love of recording audio books comes from my narration work in TV documentaries, and from understanding how important the narrator is to carry the viewer along the structure of the program.

The interesting thing is, that when the pictures are taken away from a television documentary into an audio only format, it is the skill of the narrator to actually create those missing pictures in the listener's head, turning the expert words of the author into sound. And later in the course, we'll explain more about this, and how you can create pictures in the listener's heads for both fiction and non-fiction books.

(Katy Brody writing this) And I'm a huge consumer and narrator of audiobooks! As children, we all loved being read stories to, and as adults it's a way of getting back into the comforting days of childhood. But as a mother as well as a voice artist, I'm also well aware that if your heart isn't into the reading, the listeners can "tune out" quite quickly; more on that later!

We'll also explain how you need to work with the author to adapt the text and how it's read to work better in an audio format.

We'll explain about the way you need to approach the text, and how to keep in mind the listener at all times. A mistake that some beginners to audiobook narration make is that they forget that the listener hasn't as much information as they have.

Before recording, you as the narrator, would have at least skim-read through the book, and have got a sense of where it is going, and you would have of course the text in front of you on the screen as you record it.

For listeners, they have only your voice in their head to follow what's going on, so not only does the vocal delivery need to be crystal clear, but you need to let the sense of what you're saying sink in. In the next section, we'll explain the 3 "P's" of audiobook   production.

9 - THE 3 "P'S" OF AUDIOBOOK PRODUCTION

 **FICTION BOOKS**

 **NON- FICTION / FACTUAL BOOKS**

So why aren't all audiobooks narrated by the actual authors? Well for most of the classics, it's rather difficult for these authors to narrate anything - because they're dead, but for contemporary books, audio versions that are read by the actual author are actually rare; it's not always that authors haven't the skills or the right kind of voice, often it's because they feel out of their comfort zone in a recording studio, or maybe they haven't the time to record as the pressure is on to write their next project!

So that leaves a lot of work for us, voice actors, but the first thing we'd say to you is to make sure you have the time to devote to audiobook recording. You need to be committed, dedicated and professional and not be prone to distraction. Even for a short story audio book of say, an hour, you are looking at a good 2 hours or more of solid work, and more if it's a factual technical or medical book where you have to stop regularly to check pronunciations, or if it's a fiction project full of different character voices. You can't "just knock off 10 minutes' worth" before breakfast and come back to it later. Your voice will change, your mood will change, the different sections won't edit together successfully, trust me, and they really won't.

Now we assume that you already have a decent recording set-up or voice booth on hand to record your audio books. But don't worry if you are completely new to all of this type of work. Towards the end, we do have a complete section on how to set up an audio recording facility, your own studio, in the comfort of your home, for a range of budgets.

Let's sum up the whole audiobook production process: First, as we know, there are two types of audiobooks, in the same way as there are two types of books; fiction or non-fiction, or as we'll call them in this course, "factual". Many approaches will be the same for both types, but we'll also have plenty on specific issues and tips for both.

The audiobook process is in three parts – the three "P's" – PREPARATION, PERFORMANCE & PRODUCTION.

The Preparation work includes agreeing the fee, choosing the narrator if you're a producer not voicing it yourself, choosing the voice styles for the characters and then adapting the whole manuscript for audio use. This may mean cutting chunks out that don't make sense in an audio format or changing the text so it does. We'll explain the details later.

The Performance is the recording process itself with the narrator. For bigger budget audiobooks, often the narrator will be just that; the producer or director will cast the most appropriate voice talent, they'd work with the author to adapt the original print or Kindle version for audio use, and the voice actor will be directed in the studio for the recording sessions. After the recording, the hired voice goes away and it's up to the producer and their team of editors and mixers to get the final product that consumers will get to listen to via one of the many audiobook platforms.

For smaller budgets, it is perfectly possible for it to be a one-person job, to get the manuscript from the author, adapt it for audio in association with the author, to record it and to edit and master the files, all to a very high standard, and all from the comfort of your own home, and all done by you.

So, if it's you wearing all the hats, and that's the way we like to work, actually, you'll not just be narrating, but also be responsible for editing and mastering the recorded material in the Production part of the three "P" part process.

10 - WHAT MAKES A GREAT AUDIOBOOK NARRATOR?

This section is about the skills and attributes of a good audiobook narrator. If you're already an established voice artist, then really you should be able to hit the ground running with audiobooks, however it may be a bit of a shock that you can't complete jobs as quickly! If you're used to recording short scripts such as corporate image films, radio commercials, basically projects that can be fully completed in 20 minutes to half an hour, it's going to be a big change to have endless pages to cope with, and knowing that you'll have to be consistent in voice delivery for days or even weeks!

Of course if you are a professional with plenty of stamina and you follow the advice that we're giving you, you should be fine, but I think the most difficult thing for someone to come to terms with concerning audiobook narration for the first time, is the temptation to stop the audiobook recording as soon as another – seemingly more urgent voice job comes in - or if they simply get distracted by something else. Even the best written book can get a bit tedious to work on at times and to take a break "just to quickly record" that short radio ad that has just arrived in your "in box" looks very tempting! But do you really want to fall behind on your delivery schedule?

The key thing to do is to develop a strict "Audiobook Mindset". You need to box off part of the day when you are going to do nothing else but audiobook work. Just ring-fence that time period! It shouldn't be that difficult to do for established voice over talents, because when you are being directed by a client live over headphones, you don't look at emails then do you? You don't start doing your accounts or order online groceries do you in a down-the-line session, do you? So as we say, develop a mindset of it being "an exam" in a way. Pretend you are back at school or college, sat in a very quiet exam hall where you're not allowed to talk to anyone else or be distracted by anything so your full concentration is on the task in hand.

The other thing is, if you keep on stopping and starting, you may forget where you are, and when you pick up, your voice may certainly change how it was before, so you really have to watch out for that consistency change.

So apart from this new discipline, what other skills are needed? You need to be a very good sight reader, and one where you can be flexible. Narration and voiceover is not just reading aloud in "a nice voice". Emotions often need to change as the text progresses, and character voices have to allude to the mood or emotion the person who is speaking is experiencing. For short average voiceover scripts, you can of course stop and start and the final edit could consist of various "takes" cut together. For audio book narration, you simply won't have time for this. You won't – honestly! People who start out in voiceover narration have ideas of reading the book all the way through at normal speed, underlining emphasis words, or highlighting sections of text in different colors to represent the different moods and emotions, but honestly this will massively increase your workload and often results in pretty ham acting. The best, fastest and most natural way is to learn to sight-read – yes, right "off the page"…not just so you don't trip up on the actual words, but so you can glance ahead and know how your voice is going to have to change.

If you've ever read to a child at bedtime, you wouldn't pre-read or rehearse that night's Peter Rabbit book, or whatever, would you? You'd pick it up, and it's kind of obvious for anyone how lines should be read, and usually, for young children, the more "over the top" the delivery, the better the reaction and enjoyment of the story that you're reading. So, for adult book narration, you need to train yourself to sight-read in a similar manner, glancing ahead so you'll know how your narration style and emotion should change relating to the content and situation.

Should your voice be poignant....angry...reflective.... menacing...you get my drift. Your sight reading should also instruct your brain to adapt your voice for volume, pace, tone, knowing where to pause. It sounds a lot to do, but it's perfectly possible; if WE can train ourselves, you can as well! You do this by practice; read aloud as much as you can. If you're a complete beginner, you can read aloud to yourself, or volunteer in your community to read stories at a play group, an old folk's home, or you can volunteer to record talking newspapers for the visually impaired.

11 - MORE ON BOOSTING SIGHT READING SKILLS

The more you read aloud, and ideally also record and play back so you can monitor your performance so you can improve, the better you'll get at sight reading. Of course you'll always get some sentence construction or a missing punctuation issue where it's not obvious what the sense is, and you'll need to stop and pick up, but you need to get to a stage of being able to pick a random book on a shelf, open any page and start narrating to a very high standard.

The other advantage of reading more and more, is that your vocabulary will improve. Years ago, my boss at the radio station where I was a presenter at, thought I should expand my on-air vocabulary. He told me that I had to find a new word each day, write it in a book with its meaning and use it on that day's radio show, without it being obvious. That tip has paid off so well over the years! So when you get to a word that an author has used that you're not quite sure how to say it or what it means, stop and use a pronunciation site like Forvo.com or HowJSay.com; but also click on the MEANING as well, as that will help you remember it for the future.

Another skill for the audiobook narrator is to understand English grammar. But why, you may say? Isn't that for the writer to sort out? Well, yes, but if you, the narrator, also understand English grammar to a high standard, you'll also know how you can break some grammar rules for speaking – conversational English is so different from formal written English - so if you need to brush up on your "subject" and "predicate" of a sentence; "clauses" and "parts of speech", then do so, as it will really help you in the long run. Do you know when to say "THUR" and when you say "THEE"? You see, with grammar, you'll get to a stage where you won't need to remember the actual rules, things will just "sound wrong", as you listen to your performance as you record.

At the end of the day, the narration should sound natural and pleasant for the listener to hear as well as being fully connected to the type of book and the situation you're narrating. Ask yourself at all times: "If I were listening to this, would I relate to what's going on? Would I understand what is being narrated? Would I know which character is speaking now?

The way you do this at all times is to continually monitor yourself, you need to carefully listen while you carefully speak! With audiobooks, you need to have a very acute sense of listening to what you are speaking, because unless you've got a colleague who is listening to your every word to check that you haven't made any mistakes or to stop you to suggest better ways of delivering a sentence or section, it's just you on your own.

Yes, you COULD of course play back everything you record on the loudspeakers to check after recording each chapter, but that would eat up a lot of time in your day. Voiceovers need to be totally confident that what they've recorded is accurate and clear before sending files to clients. Do you really want to send off chapters to your client and then have a long list of notes with mistakes and errors and omissions and bad pronunciations that all have to be fixed?

If you think just the recording and editing of long form voice work is tiring, just wait until you have to REPAIR your recordings - maybe weeks into the future when you've forgotten much of the project. But don't worry, fixing mistakes is quite easy if you train the client the right way, and we'll mention that later on!

So how do you listen carefully to what you're actually speaking at the same time? You need to develop a mental technique that we call it the "three head" monitoring system.

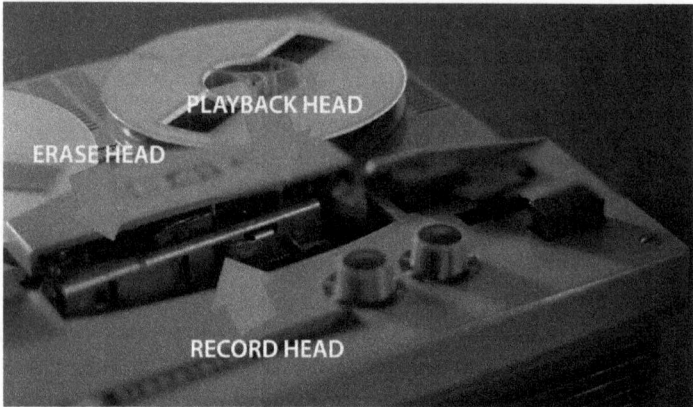

This may seem mad to you, but it works for me. Old reel-to-reel tape recorders used to have three magnetic heads. As the reels spun round, firstly the magnetic tape passed over the erase head – here you have to imagine you are "erasing your mind" to stop any distracting thoughts coming in; then there's the second head – the record head of the tape recorder – you are recording the words off the screen, and then there is the third magnetic head, the "play" or "monitor" magnetic head, where you are listening intently to what you are actually saying to make sure that what you have said is correct and also is said in a correct WAY with clarity and with all the right characteristics, such as correct accent, emotion, power and so on. Like on an old-fashioned tape recorder, you need to train yourself to do all these three things effectively at the same time. It IS possible! Just think like an old tape recorder!

Narrators need to
CAREFULLY LISTEN
as they
CAREFULLY SPEAK

This is the technique you need to train yourself to do, and it is totally possible, you are effectively LISTENING CAREFULLY at the same time as you are SPEAKING CAREFULLY!

If you find this difficult to master, try using headphones, listing to your voice without any latency or delay, at the same time that you're speaking. If you've ever worked in the radio industry, you will have to wear headphones anyway, particularly when you're listening to what your producer is saying, without it coming on the air, or to deal with phone calls without feedback happening. When you are a voice over, sometimes wearing headphones helps you enunciate better, because it amplifies the sound in your head. If you can't get on with wearing both ears on, try putting one headphone on the ear and the other one not on, and some people like this. But most people to be honest, can cope without headphones at all, and it's much more comfortable, especially for long recording sessions.

So that's the talent you need, but what about the equipment? Again if you're already an established voice-over with your own recording facility, you don't need anything else apart from a very comfortable voice booth, as you will be there a long time! For short scripts, many people prefer to stand up, but I doubt if you would want to stand up to record hours and hours of narration, no matter how interesting it is.

So if you have a stand-only booth, you will almost certainly find yourself desperate for a seat, so you will need to convert your booth and the height of the screen to accommodate this. Generally your scripts will come on a Microsoft Word or PDF file format, and so you will need a decent mouse with a scroll wheel to move the script up, but you must get one that is quiet. The last thing people want to hear is your nasty ratcheting scroll wheel working in the background!

If you haven't got your own recording facility yet, and you just want to start off recording audiobooks, that's no problem whatsoever, and in a later section we'll look at choosing equipment and setting up your audio recording studio at home.

12 - GETTING PAID FOR AUDIOBOOKS - FEES AND AGREEMENTS

❧

STAGED PAYMENTS TO NARRATOR / PRODUCER

PAYMENT # 1 - At start of project (before recording)

PAYMENT # 2 - Halfway stage

PAYMENT # 3 - End of recording

PAYMENT # 4 - After all pickups and after ACX
or the dstribution platform ahve accepted the files

In this section, we'll look in detail at the various scenarios of an author or publisher working directly with an audiobook narrator, and also how online platforms such as ACX, Findaway Voices and Author's Republic operate.

Assuming you are a freelance narrator and have been approached by an author or publisher, you need to ascertain two main things:

How much you'll be paid…and when you'll be paid!

Wouldn't it be awful to spend weeks recording an audiobook and then never get paid for the work? With ACX and other established platforms, they keep funds and distribute them when the work is done. More these systems soon. But if you are independently working for someone, as a freelancer narrator and producer, here is what we suggest.

You need to know if the author or publisher are prepared to sign an agreement that includes payments and delivery dates, as well as details of rights assigned, and any royalty arrangements.

Also you need, as the narrator, the "clean" version of the whole manuscript. The author needs to understand that an audiobook can't just be recorded with the extract text, word-for-word from the physical or Kindle book. We'll have more details about this in the next section, but basically, an audiobook has – of course - no illustrations and if there are references to these in the text, the text needs to be adapted, ideally by the author so you, the narrator doesn't get it wrong. The narrator also would not read out the index or the legal publishing page either with ISBN number, and so on. That's why we always send out an adapted and personalized version of the following document, and you're welcome to download it and use it yourself:

NOTE: *This document is intended to be a useful template for voice actors and audiobook narrators and is intended to be sent to the author or publisher of the book you are about to record and produce. You are welcome to adapt it in any way. The document is provided "as is", and we are not responsible for any misunderstandings or legal action taken if you misuse this communication.*

Dear (Author's name)

As I'm sure you'll appreciate, any physical or Kindle book needs to be slightly adapted for audiobook recording, as an audiobook listener cannot see any visuals such as photos, graphics or speech marks. Do you wish to create an "audio-friendly" version, or will you let me adapt the manuscript for you with minor adjustments? For example, I will not usually narrate any references to photographs or illustrations; I will not narrate the index or the dedication page or any of the legal publishing information that is in the printed version of the book. Do you need "About the Author" recorded at the end?

I also notice that the chapters of your book have titles, but no chapter numbers, so I will assign chapter numbers to go with the chapter names to assist the ACX audiobook upload process and to help the user navigate the chapters. Is that OK?

Maybe you wish to go through the whole manuscript and slightly adjust certain scenes for audio use; if so please let me know, and advise when the fully checked audio version of the manuscript will be delivered ready for recording in my studio.

Could you please give me a few sentences about the main speaking characters in the book please? Let me know their approximate age, the type of person they are and any relationships they have with other characters? Let me know any style of voice or accent you have got in mind for any of the characters. You are welcome to send links for me to hear by other actors on YouTube etc., if it helps.

I would also need to know how to pronounce your character's names and also place names that are not obvious. Please could you kindly send an audio recording saying slowly these names? Many thanks.

(LIST OF ANY UNUSUAL NAMES)

Unless you tell me otherwise, I will record and edit and master the files to the standard ACX technical specifications. These are as follows:

There will be a standard Intro credit and Outro credit file supplied using the official ACX script:

Intro credit: This is (title of book) written by (author) narrated by (narrator).

Outro credit: This has been (Title) written by (Author) narrated by (Narrator) copyright (Year) by (Author / Publisher). Production copyright (year) by (author / publisher)

The technical standard of the files that I will provide, unless you specify anything different will be:

16 bit mp3 audio files 192Kb/sec; 44.1 KHz sampling. Normalized to -3dB with light multiband compression. No music or sound effects.

Every file to start with half a second of silence, at the end of each file to end with 3 to 5 seconds of silence.

Please forward the full manuscript when it's finalized and I'll offer my best quote and an agreement about rights and exact delivery dates of the chapters. However, if you commission me today, I can promise to deliver all recordings by (DATE) at the latest.

I look forward to working with you on this project.

Best wishes (NARRATOR / AUTHOR)

Then there's the actual agreement that needs to be sent to the author, if you're working direct. Don't forget this form or agreement could be generated the other end, by the author, and sent to the narrator and producer, as long as both sides agree, it doesn't matter. Again you're welcome to adapt our version for your own use, and we are not responsible for any omissions that may be relevant for your own position or circumstance, we offer the agreement "as is".

NOTE: *This document is intended to be a useful template for voice actors and audiobook narrators and is intended to be sent to the author or publisher of the book you are about to record and produce. You are welcome to adapt it in any way. The document is provided "as is", and we are not responsible for any misunderstandings or legal action taken if you misuse this communication.*

Narrator Agreement and Contract

Between (Narrator / Producer)
And (Author / Publisher)
Project name:
Date:

1) (Narrator name) is a professional voiceover based and is independent, with no exclusive agent or representation of any kind. Contacts and payments shall be made directly with him. He/She is based in (Country) and is not / is at present registered for Value Added Tax (VAT).

2) (Narrator / Producer name) has sent a recording of a free, no-obligation sample of the project to you. This agreement and contract is for you to agree that you would like him to either:

   a) Continue to record the rest of the project in this style.

   b) Offer extra editorial and technical direction another sample page will be recorded. This second demo is still free. Third and subsequent sample pages will be charged at $ X US.

If you are not happy with the sample selection, there is no obligation to continue and you can ignore this agreement and contract.

3) (Narrator) shall render performer's services in connection with this engagement in a cooperative and professional manner to the best of a performer's ability, and subject to producer's direction and control.

4) The fee for the recording, editing, optimization (using Adobe Audition) and the sending of the files to you is as follows:

(NUMBER OF WORDS) / 2.4 = (X)

$X / 60 / 60 = Y$ = Amount of hours, the duration of whole audiobook. Total cost = Y x (Hourly rate) = $Z

4 staged payments are asked for as follows, about a quarter at these stages: PAYMENT 1 – START OF RECORDING: $Z / 4

PAYMENT 2 – MID POINT OF RECORDING: $Z / 4

PAYMENT 3 – END OF RECORDING: $Z / 4

PAYMENT 4 – AFTER COMPLETION OF RE-RECORDS: $Z / 4

5) Files shall be delivered by internet file transfer as either way, aif or ACX compliant mp3 files. After 14 days, if the master files are required again, an extra fee of $X shall be required.

6) The fee for this project includes full "buy-out" with no future monies being requested or demanded in the future. The "buy out" includes selling on, downloading, duplicating on flash media, CD and DVD, as well as encoding in software, apps, devices and in public announcement machinery for perpetuity.

7) With the rights of the voiceover recording given over 100% to the client, (Narrator / Producer) shall not be held liable in

any way for any legal action as a result of the content of the material being broadcast or distributed such as the script causing offence or breaching copyright in any way.

8) The client confirms that they do own the full legal rights over the text material (Narrator / Producer) has been asked to record.

9) (Narrator / Producer) agrees to complete the project in 3 working days, assuming he has the full and final script. Any re-takes due to errors in the script or in changing style by the client(s) will be charged for again at the normal rate.

Agreed by Author / Publisher

Signed:

Signed:

NARRATOR / PRODUCER

So in an ideal world, the author or publisher will send over to the narrator and / or producer the version of the manuscript ready for audio book recording, a pronunciation guide if required, and details of any characters who have voices in the book.

Also the author receives the first invoice out of four, or whatever has been agreed, and that is paid before the narrator starts to record at their end.

So that's all well and good, but what about when the author has posted auditions on an online platform, how do the payments work then, when you're not working direct?

13 - ALL ABOUT ACX – AUDIOBOOK CREATION EXCHANGE

Let's discuss the Audiobook Creation Exchange platform - ACX.com. ACX at the time of recording covers the United States, Canada, the United Kingdom, and Ireland. If you are an author, you have various options when you work with an ACX. You can post your book there and search for a narrator and producer of your work. You can listen to various samples from narrators who have posted samples on the website, or you can actually put your book up for audition, and ask people to record about 10 to 15 minutes of your book, and you can choose the best voice for your project.

Once you have chosen a narrator, you can choose between exclusive royalty where you will earn 40% of retail sales income on platforms like Audible, Amazon and iTunes and you get exclusive distribution. Or you can choose non-exclusive royalty system, this means that you have the right to distribute your audiobook elsewhere and you earn 25% of retail sales on Audible, Amazon and iTunes.

When it comes to recording the actual audiobook, if you are an author and you don't want to record or produce it yourself, there are two choices here as well. You can either pay your narrator and producer a one-time fee option such as $200 or $300 per finished hour of audio and you collect full royalties. By the way, they emphasize that is a rate per finished hour and not the hours you work on the project! Or you may want to pay nothing at all, share your future royalties with the narrator & producer.

If you're thinking of taking a royalty share, and be paid nothing initially for all the work, I think it's really important to see how successful the author is, with the book that you are about to narrate and produce. So if the book is already available on Amazon or Kindle, look up to see how many reviews it has had, look at the star rating, what people are saying about it, the buzz about the book on social media, and ask yourself what your gut feeling is about it. But of course, a big seller on Kindle or in print version doesn't necessarily mean an audio version would be a success does it? If the book has lots of photos or diagrams in, or books of many quotes, or recipe books and so on, these have been proven not to work well in an audio format, so it may be best to not go for a royalty profit share here.

If you think that it IS going to be a big seller, then go for the royalties, and I've had books I am still earning royalties monthly that were recorded many years ago and I am earning far more than if I accepted the "buy out" $200 – or whatever - per hour option. If you're not that certain, then insist on the buyout option where you're paid "per finished hour" and that's it, no royalties. Whether you are an author, publisher, narrator, or producer, or all four, you can read full details on the ACX.com website.

Another advantage of working for ACX is that there is a Bounty Referral Program, where you can earn up to $75 each time a new Audible listener becomes a member using the referral link sent from you and you get this bounty money in addition to any royalties earned from the sale of your audiobook book.

Now, if you're an author looking to find a narrator or to distribute your audiobook, you don't have to use ACX, there are other aggregators and platforms out there. The main ones are AUTHORS REPUBLIC and FINDAWAY VOICES. FINDAWAY VOICES distribute your audio book, via Hoopla and Overdrive, for library distribution and Barnes and Noble and Audible for consumers.... but also if you want to look for a narrator and producer as well, like with ACX, you can do this on this platform as well.

FINDAWAY VOICES have a feature called Voice Share, where you can share royalties between author and narrator. Also, if your book starts to do very well, you can buy out your option! FINDAWAY have a good distribution deal with Apple too. However AUDIBLE is the largest Audiobook Company out there, so you may want to go direct to ACX rather than paying an aggregator.

If you're an author weighing up the options, read the small print of each platform very carefully as some platforms are better for some types of audiobooks than others. Also you may live in a country which ACX does not recognize, so you may not have the option to use acx.com and HAVE to use an aggregator. If you are in a country that ACX can work with, as we said, the United States., Canada, the United Kingdom and Ireland you need to have a full home address in one of those locations, tax ID, and a bank account in one of those countries that it works with.

14 - AUDIOBOOK PREPARATION

Before any narrator takes on a new project, it's important to look at the whole audiobook text as provided from the author, or publisher. You may have passed an audition using only a small part of the total text, but you need to see everything, the whole manuscript, to make sure that the rest of the book is written to a similar standard and doesn't have later chapters with very hard-to-read or difficult terms, or characters that would be difficult to bring to life.

Once you have the full manuscript, make sure you insist on getting the Microsoft Word version of it and not a locked PDF file. This is so you can easily change the font for your recording booth so you can change it to a size and style of font that you personally find easy to read. Also you may want to separate paragraphs more, or to put in notes to yourself in brackets after you have gone through the book.

So once you have the full manuscript, do you have to read it all? You can if you wish to, but to be honest you don't need to read every word. You can skim read and you can train your mind to look out for difficult words or passages. If it was a physical book, it should take you about 30 seconds at most to skim-read each page. For a full screen page of text, about a minute. Make a note of the page numbers that you have concerns about. Then, before recording, you would write to the author or publisher and ask how certain words are pronounced all that you don't understand the certain paragraph or any other concerns you have. So the answer to the question do you need to read it all, no you don't need to read it like someone enjoying the book would read it, but you are scanning it as professional, so that any issues do not surprise you in the recording session if you have to stop recording to ask a question author, this will really mess up your workflow big-time. Yes, you could leave a gap, come back to it later, what if you forego the many other areas you need to come back later you have heard back from the author? Why give yourself all this grief and extra work? So preparation is really key before you record anything.

Professional authors should create different versions of their work for audio recording. For example, many factual books have graphs and photographs in that are referred to in the text of the book, which would make absolutely no sense in an audio book version would it? So these would need to be removed. We sometimes get sent "refer to the diagram" and so on in factual scripts these will have to be taken out.

This is why it is important to get the whole manuscript. If the author asks you to make up your own mind as to what goes in and stays, or refuses to send you anything other than a PDF file that you cannot easily adapt even with Adobe Acrobat, and what's more they don't want to pay you more to adapt the script, then usually it's best to walk away from the project, because it sounds like the author will be high maintenance, they do not understand your needs, and you'll end up spending much more time in edit when the author doesn't agree with any changes you have made. Basically, what we are saying is that author or publisher must completely sign up to helping produce the audiobook version and make it very clear to you what is to be read and what is not to be read.

Here are some other questions to ask the author. Do they really want the acknowledgements read by the narrator? What about all the various dedication's, or quotes that you sometimes get on flysheets of books. Surely, they don't want the whole index recorded?! I hope not!

In factual or non-fiction, quite often authors use a term to describe something that's been explained or mentioned before and they use the rather old-fashioned "as discussed above". Well, "above" would be in a textbook, but it's sort of "before" in an audiobook isn't it? But do you need this at all? So all these things need to be changed in the script before recording anything.

But where things get much more confusing, is when there are people talking to each other. In fiction audiobooks, we often see situations on manuscripts where people are talking to each other but unless you can see the speech marks, it's confusing for the listener to know who exactly is saying what line and to whom!

Quite often the author won't say "…. John said", or "Steve replied", because it gets a bit

tedious after a while. So in a pretty long conversation, you will just get set a person's piece of speech followed by the other person's piece of speech with just switch marks around them. That's ok if you can see the speech marks, but if you can't the author will need to tell you what they want to do in a situation like that.

If the author is not around anymore to tell you, then you've got to take things into your own hands! If there are two people talking to each other this is where your character voices really have to be well distinguished apart. In some books it's quite easy.

If you're recording a Bertie Wooster book from the 1920's for example as I've done in the past, a jaunty "Stephen Fry" style narration would be fine for Bertie and the butler, Jeeves would be totally different. The author, PG Wodehouse, often used the device of one character's line followed by the other character in a conversation; but the poor audio listener can't see the speech marks. So you need to make it clear in your narration.

I put all this to Jeeves:

"Odd, his coming to me. Still, if he did, he did. No argument about that. It must have been a nasty jar for the poor perished when he found I wasn't here."

"No, sir. Mr. Fink-Nottle did not call to see you, sir."

"Pull yourself together, Jeeves. You've just told me that this is what he has been doing, and assiduously, at that."

"It was I with whom he was desirous of establishing communication, sir."

"You? But I didn't know you had ever met him."

"I had not had that pleasure until he called here, sir. But it appears that Mr. Sipperley, a fellow student of whom Mr. Fink-Nottle had been at the university, recommended him to place his affairs in my hands."

The mystery had conked. I saw all. As I dare say you know, Jeeves's reputation as a counsellor has long been established among the cognoscenti, and the first move of any of my little circle on discovering themselves in any form of soup is always to roll round and put the thing up to him.

Did you notice on the video in the course how I tackled this? It's a trickier book to turn into audio form that you'd think, and PG Wodehouse is not around to help me adapt it into a good audio format. First you have Bertie Wooster as the narrator, then there is Bertie speaking to Jeeves, his butler. Then in the conversation in the middle, there are only speech marks, which the audio listener cannot see, so there is no "I said" or "Jeeves retorted" or so on. So, your voice has to do all the work.

The Bertie Wooster narration I did closer to the mike, and then for when Bertie was in the conversation, I pulled my head away from the microphone as if I was the other side of the room having my discourse with Jeeves. Then you've just got to keep Bertie "jaunty" and Jeeves in his British butler-style, almost bored timbre! Of course, with two characters that are wildly different it is fairly straight forward, but things get more complicated when you have two or three people talking together who have similar voice styles and all accents. You can of course, make one character speak a little slower than the others, and one with a type of emotion that is unique to them, but we will do more on characters later.

So what about pictures and photographs? I have worked with some authors who actually want me to mention about pictures, graphs and photographs in the text version of the book. Cleverly, they've worked out that if listeners have enjoyed the audio version of the book, they may want to buy the text version as well as a reference, where you can get all the pictures and graphs and visuals that have been mentioned. Of course in the audio version of the book, it gets a bit tedious to not say "have a look at the photograph on page 23" and replace it with "on page 23 of the text version of this audiobook..." so that's another conversation will   you   and   the   author.

15 - FACTUAL AUDIOBOOK NARRATION VOICE STYLE

So what sort of narration voice should be used for your audiobook? With a factual, non-fiction book, you need to try and imagine the type of person who would be listening. Remember, that you are just speaking to one person, who is listening intently to you. So, imagine the ideal person who would be listening to it. The person who bought that factual audiobook, because they are really very keen to learn more about the subject matter. Imagine that person, imagine how they are reacting to your words. It is really important to try and target your ideal listener, and you will then structure the whole of your performance to that person, even if they are imaginary.

One of the audiobooks would for example be about the history of the Berlin Airlift – the rescue deliveries for the people of Berlin when the soviets stopped supplies. So here we assume the person listening to the audiobook would already be an avid watcher of historical factual programs on TV, so a standard BBC style documentary was perfect for this.

Another one was about Forex trading, here it needed to be much more upbeat and modern as the book had plenty of facts and information for the listener to put into action. You needed to image a keen person who just wanted the facts to get started trading.

Many audiobooks are educational of course; at the time of recording, I've just completed three very long instructional audiobooks for people who are training to be licensed insurance agents in Canada. Also last year, I voiced a very academic audiobook about block chain. For any educational work, you need to be very clear about the facts and information to be emphasized and to slow down over important areas, and the use of pauses to let information sink in is very important.

A trick that many voice talents use when imparting information, whether it's in a documentary, or in a training video is the sound like you are a real expert on the subject matter, when quite often you aren't, and almost certainly you hadn't written the script yourself.

So you can try and understand the subject matter, but often it's so complicated and very specialized, so it's almost impossible to fully understand it.

The technique is to emphasize what seemed to be the obvious words, to make you sound like you're the expert. the problem is, and this especially happens with long form audio, when you're narrating a very long factual audio book, you get into a system of emphasizing most adjective's on autopilot, and you can make some terrible mistakes if you're not careful.

So with non-fiction, factual books, are there character voices? Sometimes, when there are quotes from people.

Quite often, by the way, you may have to reverse the name attribution. You may have a quote from a politician or soldier, or whatever, and in the written version of the book you have the quote before the name of the person who said the quote is printed below it. That's fine for a book, as we all scan the author of the quote at the bottom before we read a quote, don't we? In the world of audio, we can't do this!

For an audiobook, you need to put it the other way round, particularly if it's a long quote. So instead of a long quote and then at the end you say that's what Oscar Wilde said, or whatever, you would change it around so that you'd say Oscar Wilde once said, and then say the actual quote.

That way the listener doesn't get confused, especially for long quotes. So, again, you often have to tweak the script for audiobook recording use, with the permission of the author or publisher.

16 - FICTION AUDIOBOOK NARRATION VOICE STYLE

With a fiction audiobook, you need to take a totally different approach to factual books, as it's usually not just one voice that you have to perform. As well as playing the part of the narrator, in your normal voice, each of the characters needs to have a unique type of voice. Now to the listener, they know it's really just you speaking, but you just need to give a nod to the unique character of each person who is speaking.

So if you're a male voice-over, when a female is speaking, you may want to raise the pitch a bit, clip the voice, and find a suitable pre-set using our "Character Control Panel" mentioned earlier. For other characters, the author may give you specific guidance, and even send you links to YouTube videos they want you to emulate; but, as we've mentioned before, they've got to sound different from each other.

So, one person may sound sort of vaguely bored all the time, one person is generally perky and enthusiastic, someone is sarcastic, one person has a northern accent, one person speaks very slowly, one person may be hyper active, you get the drift. So how do you assign voices to the characters, and how do you know how many characters there are? That is why, unless your author has kindly provided this information, you need to speed-read the whole manuscript.

Flick through it and write down a list of all the characters who are going to speak. If you don't do this, and just start at the very beginning and put a lot of effort into that first chapter and the initial characters, and give them your best voices, how would you know that that first person you've just given your best voice to, is not killed off in chapter 2?!

Also you may find that if you can only do one Cockney accent for example, there are three other characters that need a Cockney accent that come in the second half, and somehow they've got to sound slightly different from each other!

So ideally you would record a little clip of each of the voices before you even start recording the main narration, and keep the audio sample files stored with their name, so you can be reminded of the sound of the voice every time you come to it. After a few chapters, you may not need to refer to the sample files, but it's important to do this. The visual element is also important here. If the author has given you any pictures or drawings of the characters – maybe book cover artwork, then pin it up in your studio. For a similar kind of work, voice acting for video games, you're often given 3D mock-up of each character to get a feel of how the character will look on screen with your voice!

So you've looked through your book and you have a list of characters there and you have to assign a different voice to every character, so they sound slightly different from each other, what do you do? First of all, don't get too hung up about it.

Everybody who is listening knows it's just you. It's not as if they're expecting to hear a radio play with different actors coming in to speak the lines. So, mellow out, and don't concern too much about making the voices very dramatically different.

18 - RECORDING CHARACTER VOICES IN THE VOICE BOOTH

Earlier, with our "Character Control Panel", we learnt how to create different and distinct character voices, but once you've assigned a voice to a character, how do you practically record them in the booth?

You see, some people have rather difficult times doing this and they find that once they've got their mind into a certain character voice, they get this idea in their head that they should record all those specific lines first while they're in the mood and "in character," and then edit them in later on. If you really want to do this, you can try it, but I bet you won't do it again! It will take an awful long time.

What would be easier for you to be honest, is to just leave a gap after you've done your character voice line...and then think of your trigger word or phrase to get you into the other person that character is talking to, and then leave another gap to try and get yourself back into the first character again.

Then in edit, of course, chop the rubbish out. Do you see what I mean? If you just did one recording with just that characters lines throughout the whole chapter or even the whole book, it would take you forever to chop them in, and it would be very hard to make it sound realistic as well. It will be far easier just to leave a gap and edit out the gaps afterwards which only takes half a second in an editing program.

If you had to find takes on another file and then cut and paste them into your master file, it really would take a very long time. Right, stay with us, and in the next video, we'll show you how to get into the right mindset for successful recordings.

19 - MINDSET – GETTING INTO THE ZONE

So, everything has been sorted out! Hoorah! The main script preparation stage is successfully completed, you've created and assigned character voices, and you are sat in your voice booth ready to narrate the first part of the project. You may have many hours and hours ahead of you, and the following sections offer some solid gold tips we hope you'll take up, in order to be efficient and to get consistent professional recordings.

As we have mentioned before, you need to get into the mindset. Come to terms with the fact that for at least the next hour or two you are just going working on the audiobook and will do nothing else. Pretend you are sat in an exam room if you like, don't be distracted by anything else. You need to be totally absorbed by the job. So, your phone needs to be switched off and, on your computer monitor you'll have nothing but the script and a browser to look up word pronunciations but your emails will be closed! For a busy freelancer hungry for work of course this could be very difficult for you. But don't worry you can take breaks. We suggest strongly that you don't record more than about 20 minutes at a time, so that's when you can take a break and stretch!

We also suggest that you technically have a "belts and braces" fail proof recording system. We will tell you more about this in the section about setting up the recording facility in your home, but basically you need to record on two different systems, and record simultaneously on the computer via USB interface using your software program such as Adobe Audition, and also record on a solid-state recorder as a backup. If one fails, the other is bound to still have the recording! And the other thing is that even if both fail which is like winning the lottery in reverse, at least you will only have lost 20 minutes.

We assume that the recording you have made on the computer is the one you would want to keep to save time copying from the solid-state recorder so after 20 minutes simply recording on the computer and save it as a wav file. Yes these wav files are very big and that's because there's so much information there, the 24-bit wav file for about 20-minutes would be about 100 MB, of course everything will eventually be mastered down to little compressed MP3 files in the end, but it's important to record and edit using the high quality files.

Once you have got that 20 minutes saved, and unedited by the way, you do that later, you can have a short break where will allow you to check your emails or visit the bathroom or have a stroll around for a couple of minutes and then you'll be fresh and ready to do the next 20 minutes.

This is all part of getting "into the zone". All this mental preparation is really important. If you think you can just knock off about 10 minutes or so before tea it will not sound good and it may certainly not match the next section of recording you will do, trust me! If you can, record at the same time of day each day, and you'll probably be too exhausted to be in the booth on this one project for more than 4 to 5 hours a day, and that should be put into your calculation of delivery date(s).

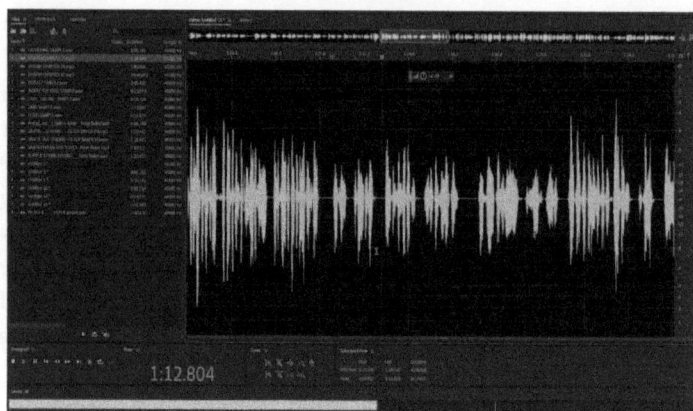

20 - BREATHING IN THE BOOTH – BANISHING NOISES

If you're a voice-over recording commercials, short promos, or anything where you need to go over it with a fine tooth comb, you will know that the smallest little imperfection has to be silenced and major breaths have to be cut out. For acting work, of course, you leave everything au naturel, breaths and all, but generally in voice-over work you clean everything up.

In the hours and hours of professional audiobook recording, you simply don't have time to do any of this. Any little rustle of your clothing, or little lip smack that shouldn't be there will just have to stay there, but that unprofessional is in it? You really won't have time to go through everything in real-time, so here is how to minimize these issues.

(Peter writing this) Whenever I go to a clothing shop, I try to make sure very quiet in there. See, I'm not just looking at the style of clothes, but also feeling the fabric if it makes a rustling sound. Something that is very minor to most human beings is a major issue for us narrators and voice-overs, where we have very sensitive large diaphragm condenser microphones and they pick up the rustle of clothing! If you have got a nice collection of soft clothes that do not make a noise when you move around, you are a very happy voice-over. If that morning you unfortunately put on a nasty shirt or top made of material that does make a noise, then simply strip off for action -hey, nobody sees you can they?

So, what about breaths in audiobooks? Even though in acting, the breaths are part of the human experience, for the narration parts of audiobooks, which will likely be 100% for factual audiobooks, you don't want too many breaths to be standing out and annoying the listener. So how can you minimize the breaths without having to spend time fixing them later in editing software? In other words, having to highlight every one of your big breaths in edit and reduce its volume, which would take ages!

So, you need keep recording and you can try to inhale big breaths in between sentences with your head away from the microphone. Think of it like swimming where your head is under the water doing a front crawl and you turn your head slightly to the side, or you can move your whole body away from the microphone in between sentences to take in a breath. This is a technique that you will learn in long-form narration.

You turn your head and take a breath and then snap your head back start the next section. The disadvantage is that maybe your eyes cannot zone in on the script when your head comes back, so you need to practice or else you may lose your place in the script. You may absolutely hate doing this, and it could give you a headache, so if this happens don't worry about it, try not moving your head to the side but the "moving the whole body back" technique. What you are aiming to do is to not take a breath with your mouth right up against the microphone capsule.

As we mentioned in our section on character voices, you should be using the distance from the microphone technique anyway. For example, when the narrator is speaking, they should be close up to the microphone, and then the character voices could be a foot away from the microphone, the actual distance really depends on the acoustics of your own recording environment. So, you are doing that with character voices to differentiate the sound of the two voices, narrator and character voice, but it's also a technique to minimize breaths as well, moving your head away from the microphone.

The other breathing technique that you may like to learn is instead of inhaling using the upper part of the chest, is to use your diaphragm muscles. When you want to take a breath in front of the microphone, push out your tummy muscles and open your mouth wide, and this sucks in air much more silently than it would do using a normal breathing technique.

Try it- is quite a useful thing to know! Yes, silent breathing!

AUDIOBOOK RECORDING
You will thank us for this tip!
- **Phone off**
- **Don't check emails**
- **Don't get distracted**

21 - USE THE POWER OF THE HUMAN MIND

We can't emphasize enough how important it is to prepare before recording anything. Wasn't it Abraham Lincoln who said "Give me an hour to cut down a tree, and I'll spend the first 59 minutes sharpening the axe?" Yes - preparation is so key to be successful recording long-form scripts, without all the hassle and pain of re-recording pages of author's feedback "notes" after you record.

Remember, your eventual aim is to record audio files to a high editorial and technical standard and to minimize any mistakes. The more mistakes you make, the time to fix them in edit will increase, so imagine you're live on stage and you just can't afford to make mistakes! If you're a professional actor, you'll know how the adrenaline kicks in to help you give great performances even if you feel under the weather or your personal life has just fallen apart that day. But that adrenaline comes from a theatre full of audience members staring at you. When you're on your own in your lonely voice booth, when you're even free to record when you like, it's never the same. But you need to believe in the power of the human mind and what it can achieve.

(Peter writing this) Many years ago I was a presenter on a radio station. I was asked to present the Sports program on a Saturday afternoon, which covered various live football matches. In my particular region of England, they were usually 4 or 5 matches played at exactly the same time. My job was to present the program live on the radio and also work the control desk covered with faders and buttons. I had to do live interviews with various people on the phone, talk to guests in the studio, play in commercials and promos and also take any of the commentators' feeds from their sports ground whenever there was a goal or something of interest like a penalty or a sending off.

Before I took the job, I assumed there would be a team of people in a nearby control room listening individually to each football ground, who would tell me, the presenter, whenever there was a goal. But, oh no! It was just me with an assistant. Between us we had to listen to live football commentary from 5 different games on our headphones and understand what was going on at each match and make a decision live on air as to whether to go over and take the feed from the commentator. We also had to record the feed from each commentator on separate reel-to-reel tape recorders in the studio, (we had no digital computers then!) and have to edit bits out of the tape, cutting with razor blades and sticking with tape, when actually talking live on air. Amazingly it all worked generally well!

The reason I am telling you this, is that from that day, I realized how incredible the human mind is, and you can train it to do so many different things at the same time. In my voice over work, I realized how much multitasking was going on here as well. So let's assume you are behind the microphone reading a long-form script like an audiobook. What is your brain actually doing?

First of all, of course there is the "third head monitoring technique" we discussed earlier. This where you train yourself to carefully listen while you carefully read!

Another task you need to ask your brain to do is to sight read – perfectly! Short scripts are easy to learn. For very long audiobook scripts, there is no way you're going to remember it all. So when reading and recording, look ahead. Let's assume that you're the driver of a car, well, you need to ask your brain to play the part of a navigator looking at …sort of "road signs" up ahead to see which ways to turn, and the speed to drive. As your eyes scan the words on the screen that you are reading at the moment, you're also looking ahead to see if any "pitfall" words are coming up, unusual words that you will have to think beforehand about how they are pronounced.

But it's not just unusual words looming up in the road ahead a part of your brain needs to think about so you don't have to stop recording in mid-flow. Your eyes are also looking out in future text blocks for "the" words, because how you pronounce the word "the" depends on whether the word after it starts with a consonant (THE) or a vowel. (THEE). You are aware of that rule are you? If not, brush up your English grammar! The cat sat on the armchair!

Good sight reading is essential also in factual books where you may get emphasis words wrong, and miss the sense completely. More on this is in the section on fatigue in the voice booth.

So, ideally, we narrators and voice actors need to be able to do read and record perfectly and naturally first time, by glancing ahead and making your brain work it out before your mouth gets to the words!

So if you're just getting into the business of narration and are worried that you won't be able to perform good multi-task sight reading, don't worry... it's just a case of training your brain to do it. Have faith that you can do it, and with practice, you will surprise yourself, like I was surprised presenting my first sports radio show doing so many complex things at once!

22 - THINKING OF THE LISTENER

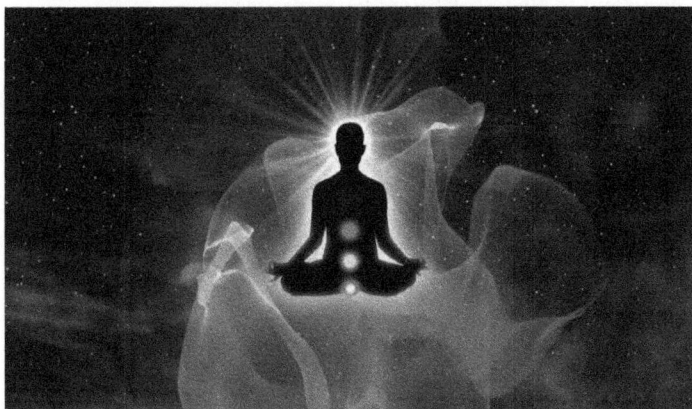

Whh you're recording, as you would with all voiceover recordings, keep in mind the typical listener to whatever type of book you're narrating. You need to think of just one person, not a group. This is something that was drummed into me when I first started in radio many years ago; any form of pluralism was banned. So a radio presenter, even though he or she knew that thousands of people were listening at that moment, would always refer to people in the singular, never the plural. So it would be never be "It looks like rain so, folks, take your umbrellas today!" You would say, (if you had to say such a line on the radio) "It looks like rain, don't forget to take your umbrella today." Even if people are listening or even watching television in a group, listeners and viewers still like to be referred to in the singular. What works in broadcasting also works for the audiobook world as well, which is even more of intimate experience.

Try and imagine the type of person who is listening, whatever type of book it is. In fact, you can try to create the "ideal listener" and you can image WHERE they are listening to your voice and what's sort the mood they are in. This may sound a bit unnecessary, but, honestly, it will really help you to focus your mind and to give a consistent performance.

Imagine the person's face, maybe someone you know, listening in their car going up and down the highway on a long journey, on a train, or maybe they are lying in bed at night listening to another chapter of your voice. This is an essential technique to really relate to the listener.

Maybe you're recording a factual book about meditation techniques; it can be incredibly helpful to think of an "ideal listener" and simply read for them, and this helps you sound "in tune" with the information even if you are sight-reading.

So you may want to read this book to a "25 year old psychology graduate who is about to embark on further studies in mediation"...or "a 40 year old divorcee who is trying to turn her life around after years of abuse from an unfaithful husband".... Or whatever.

If a friend of yours is a fan of the author whose novel you are reading, read "just for them", and you'd never believe how much extra power this gives to your longevity in the booth and by thinking this way, it's amazing how suddenly you naturally "get" what the book is about, the tone, the pace, the passion, it all comes together, you aren't simply just "reading".

23 - MAKING YOUR NARRATION AND CHARACTERS COME ALIVE

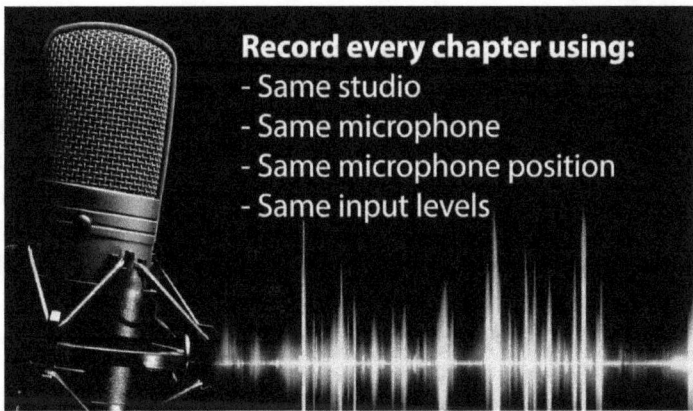

Record every chapter using:
- Same studio
- Same microphone
- Same microphone position
- Same input levels

There are two types of consistency, technical and emotional. Technical is sort of obvious really, you wouldn't record one chapter of the audio in one studio and then another chapter in another studio with a different microphone and acoustics would you? So decide where you're going to record and stick to it. Make sure that the microphone is in the same position every time, normally this is six or 7 inches away from your mouth at 45°.

Also ensure that the input levels are the same, so you get consistent levels recorded.

Emotional consistency is different. We all have different moods at different times of the day, different parts of the week, our voice is different between we are well and when we are feeling a little bit under the weather. This is where acting skills come in course and trained actors are used to putting on a wonderful performance, no matter what their underlying mood or health is.

If you don't have an acting background, a way to get over this issue is to try and record at the same time each day, and to have at least a minute or two listening back to your voice very carefully from previous sessions so you get consistency. Listen to the various elements of what you have done before, speed, the pitch in your voice, and most importantly the emotion. This consistency is for both factual or non-fiction as well as novels and other works of fiction.

Once a listener has got used to your emotional level, and have tuned into you, it is very strange when for a few chapters, you may suddenly sound more agitated, excited, or read slower or faster you have done before, when it makes no sense to the arc of the story or in the descriptions you are narrating. To make sure that your voice is the same for each new recording session, you need to get into the mood you were in the last session, so it will all edit together well.

So listen back to what you recorded last time...speak along with yourself to get the pace, the tone, the inflections, the mood. You must use the same studio, the same microphone, the same microphone placement, the same pop filter, the same chair even and of course any hardware setting must be the same for the sound to match. Why? Audiobooks leave your voice very exposed; you're not being compressed and then mixed with music and sound effects as would happen in a commercial. Many people listen to audio books via headphones, and they'll notice recording differences. If the listener doesn't, the producer or distributor will notice, and your recordings could get rejected.

A technique to use to make your work really punch above its weight, is to make the adding color to the setup passages in Fiction books. Use the tone of voice and sense of timing to really paint a picture in the listener's head of the scene where the next part of the story is about to unfurl. Certain words can be "colored" by the way you say them. So you wouldn't say flatly "The grey skies over the plains cast a gloom over the whole landscape, down to the trickling brook that wove its way to the village". You'd imagine you're there, and DESCRIBE, really coloring in the adjectives. Sound flat and bored saying "grey" and make your voice "sparkle and "trickle" saying the trickle description.

Similarly, when reading a factual book, you'd play the mental trick of pretending to be the author, the expert in the subject, no matter how unusual that may be. Try this technique, it really works!

24- SPEED, PACE AND PAUSES

Here are a few guidance notes on speed, timings and pauses. For average voice over work, with smaller scripts, you either are recording to an exact time for a TV or radio commercial, or maybe exact timings for sections over video that you are dubbing.

However, for an audio book, it's a bit like the difference between a podcast and a radio program, because can just about do what you like with the duration! The only thing to remember is that consistency is important. The listener will find it very strange if you were going much faster on one chapter for example, and that's because you are so desperate to finish it to catch a train or something! I'm sure you wouldn't be so unprofessional would you!

First factual books. Quite often factual books are actually educational books, people are trying to learn something. So you have to be very careful with the speed you're going at, to make sure that the facts and information in the script comes over well. Don't go so slow to be patronizing but also don't go too fast that you will lose people. Of course you would have made a demo or audition and the author would have told you whether they agree with your speed of reading anyway, and that's fine, and you may need to refer back to your audition before every recording session, to make sure that you are sticking to it.

The other thing with factual books where there is information to impart, is that you need to leave a little gap after every bit of important information, it doesn't have to be a huge gap, and it depends on the subject matter, but here's an example of an audio book that's training airline staff, and you're here the gaps that are just right, neither too short so it seems as if you are skipping over the information, and neither too long so people think there's a mistake in the audio book.

After you have been doing some of these for a while, it will become natural to you as to what is right, you may even get some of the pauses written in to the script , Sometimes it will be just a dash in the text, as three dots maybe, like an ellipsis, What should of course normally be used for missing words, but so many people use it to signify a pause in a script, or the author will put in brackets (a beat here), or even include a time such as "please pause 2 seconds" written into the script for you.

For fiction books it's still important to have the same pace of reading that was accepted in your original audition extract, but of course as the story develops and you get into a more relaxed scene, or even a more exciting scene here is where the pace can change. However, don't feel that you have to speed up because the action has spared up in the storyline. For example you wouldn't suddenly speed up when there's a car chase or something, you would let the action run out in people's heads, but there's no need to suddenly speed up like a football commentator or anything! That just wouldn't really work.

Where you can make a difference with speed of reading, is with the character voices, where you can assign different speeds to different characters, and that is one way of making one voice, in other words your own, to sound like many different types of people, by making their speech slow medium or fast or anywhere in between! We discussed this more in the section on character voices.

Pauses are also important in a fiction book, but not so that it gives time for information to be absorbed by a listener, but because you want to signify a passage of time maybe, or simply a dramatic pause where a character is thinking about what the other person has said. If you want you to this this may seem really complicated, but it's not when you really get into the story and you become the characters you understand why they are doing the things they are doing at that moment.

If you have a very well written book, and I hope that the author has provided you and good manuscript, then you should have no problem here, and naturally you will create the right sort of pauses and silences for the situation in the novel you are narrating.

By the way even though we say that the author may be very prescriptive with putting pauses into the audio book version of the manuscript, you may have an author who actually doesn't care and wants you to be as creative as possible.

If you know you have this kind of client, this kind of author or publisher, then go for it, this is such an enjoyable way to work, because you have the basics of the manuscript, and the creativity is in your own hands. So in a way, you can ignore the punctuation even, and flow one sentence into another, if you feel it is more natural.

And that's both for factual books and for fiction stories as well. So again, it is a completely different way of working then usual voice over work, where you really have to respect the commas the gaps and the other punctuation in a script that often is heavily timed as well. Audio books are much more fluid usually, especially if you have an author that respects the creativity of the narrator.

25 - CORRECTING NARRATION MISTAKES

If you were giving a live reading in front of a live audience, if you make a mistake, or cough, you would carry on of course. I'm sure even the great Charles Dickens had to stop and have a slurp of water at some point when he was reading his novels out in front of theatre audiences years ago.

Of course, in an audiobook, people are paying for perfection. Hopefully you would be monitoring what you are saying using our techniques and thus recording very carefully. So, when you slur a word, or stumble over something, or you hit your microphone, or anything else, you will need to rerecord that section. There are two schools of thought as to how you repair something in an audiobook if you make a mistake.

The first school of thought in my opinion is the wrong school of thought. It's called "punch and roll". Basically, in this system, once you make a mistake, you wind back the recording and play back.

As soon as you hear that you come to the point just before the mistake, you "punch in" to record again. You start speaking again immediately and you continue. Even the union British Equity say this is the best and most recommended way of dealing with mistakes in audiobooks. I was in London at one of their sessions and workshops all about audiobooks, and I couldn't believe what they were saying.

I think punch and roll is a crazy idea and takes up far more time than the system that I use which is simply leaving a long gap when you make a mistake. The thing is, after you have "punched in" and started recording again, how do you know if it was a clean edit or if it sounded natural? Using the punch and roll system, how on earth do you know if you haven't left two breaths in, or clipped a word, or if the intonation from one part of recording to another was correct?

So MY school of thought is, when you make a mistake, stop. Quietly think about why you went wrong by looking at the script in front of you again. Take a sip of water, take a few deep breaths, stretch a bit. Just for five to 10 seconds, close your eyes and go to your happy place.

You won't believe how refreshing doing this can be, in the middle of a long audio book recording. Then, open your eyes and simply repeat the last section where you can easily edit in later. You'd generally pick up at the start of a sentence or even a complete paragraph, it really depends where you are in the text. Make sure that you do leave a good gap that you'll be able to see in the audio waveform later though. Here's a long waveform of about an hour's worth...and by zooming in, you can see where the mistakes are easily. We'll tackle audio editing in detail later on.

It can be very tempting when you've made a mistake, just to "tut" a bit and then carry on. But you won't be able to see this gap clearly, and the mistake will be left in! Leave a good five to 10 second gap so you can identify the mistake area later.

You WILL need to read the whole sentence before a slip- up. If you trip just on a word, you cannot just re-record that word and hope to edit it in - it will sound very unnatural!

Now I do say you can do anything you like when you make a mistake because you're going to cut the rubbish out anyway, but a very important tip is that you should never swear in front of the microphone. I know one voice over who actually didn't like his particular client very well and ranted at the microphone about the client an awful lot during his own mistakes, and guess what, yes, he edited out all the swearing and saved it, but unfortunately sent the wrong file – the whole original unedited file to the client. So that was a bit embarrassing wasn't it? So, the number one rule is never swear in front of any microphone, even if you think it's switched off!

One other tip that might be useful to you is that when you are picking up when you've made a mistake, to beforehand explain something to yourself - or to your editor if you're not editing yourself - why you're picking up and where you're picking up from... any little notes like that are useful. But do them in a really soft voice, and not your normal presenting voice, so the waveform will look like it's a mistake and not part of the finished audio book that would be at normal volume.

So that's about it, I know we've covered an awful lot on preparation, but there's so much that has to go on in the voice booth, and there's an awful lot to learn to get really good quality recordings for hours and hours that professional and will keep the listeners attention throughout.

So put your computer into record and off you go, and I highly recommend that you also make a duplicate copy on a completely different device. A good tip is to record on the computer via your USB interface, as usual, but also to record a standby file on a solid state recorder as well. The probability of both failing is almost impossible. There is more chance of an asteroid hitting your studio from outer space! You'd do this practically by buying a "Y" shape splitter from your microphone, so one output from your mike goes into the computer, via the USB interface box, and the other goes into a solid state recorder as back-up.

Also before you switch your computer off, also make a copy on a memory stick or in the cloud, because wouldn't it be terrible if your computer didn't boot up again, or corrupted the files, or someone stole your computer in the night or whatever! So, make a copy of everything at the end of every day just to be on the safe side.

Finally, always, always, always…. remember the listener, and that will help you keep the

perfect pace of narration. Imagine their face with headphones on, totally absorbed in what you're imparting to them. Your speed of narration and leaving the right amount of gaps and pauses will help them get totally immersed in your audiobook. You are the great "storyteller", let your clear, creative, imaginative voice take your listeners by the hand into your world!

26 - AVOIDING THE FATIGUE FACTOR

As a narrator tasked with recording a long audiobook, watch the "fatigue factor". After a few hours in the voice booth, there is such a big temptation just to get into the rhythm and almost singsong delivery of everything you've done before, you are reading on "remote control" – and a part of your mind wanders to thinking what you are having for dinner tonight - and your eyes don't quite get the right words. And you say the wrong words, but your ear doesn't pick this up, simply because the sound and rhythm are the same as previous sections of recording. So the ear thinks that all is well, but it's not!

It's difficult to describe how this happens, but I've been picked up by clients where they reveal on playback that I said completely the wrong word. I thought that I recorded the one that was in the script, but because the word that I substituted had the same first two or three characters or the same sort of ending, my brain was fooled, and I didn't check, just because I was a little tired....I'd say association when it should be alleviation... or

pronounce "GRADUate" as if it were a noun when I should have said it as a verb like "graduATE". You may say "genetically" when the script said "generically"....or "assessed"

when it should have be "accessed". Do you see what I mean? That's why it's important to take breaks and maybe do another project and come back to it later - don't do more than two hours recording of an audio book at a stretch, and that's of course splitting it up into 20 minutes sections.

It's usually the emphasis words that snookers a tired audiobook narrator, especially when you're recording a non-fiction or a factual book, where if you put the wrong emphasis on a word in a sentence or a phrase, the full sense or meaning of what you're saying doesn't come across. Here's an example of a repeated word in a sentence. If you're a bit tired and reading "on autopilot", you're likely to pronounce a word wrong, like "CONtract" when you should have said "conTRACT" or to emphasize the wrong words so it will simply not make sense to the listener.

Hopefully the subject matter of the factual book you're narrating makes sense to you, so it should be obvious which words to emphasize. But sometimes you have a very technical audio book - maybe about engineering, pharmacy, or even yes, insurance, where you really are not an expert on the subject and you have no idea what words to emphasize. But with something like this you can learn to get into the groove and begin to understand the subject. This is where a good relationship with the author pays dividends as you can just call up and ask "err....what does this passage mean?

But if you specialize in audio books, and you haven't been sent any other scripts to go to of a normal "voiceover" nature, then flip flop your audio books! Get two on the go! For example at the moment I'm recording this for you, I've got a factual book in my in-tray, another one of my series about insurance, an I'm also recording an exciting detective novel , a fiction book. So it uses different parts of your brain, and it gives you a break from one style of reading to a completely different style of reading.

So what else can fight fatigue and assist your consistent delivery for the long haul? Physicality! Gestures! Moving around as you speak and doing appropriate gestures will vastly improve your delivery. Before we mention our tips here, though, a word about the scroll wheel. You need to make sure that the scrolling mouse makes the page on the screen go up at the right speed so that your eyes can read it comfortably. But what hand should you use for the mouse?

As we don't have a third hand, maybe you don't want to invest in foot pedal, although that is an option, we strongly suggest you leave your dominant hand for all the gesticulations, and use your non-dominant hand to do the simple task of running the scroll wheel to make the text go up the screen.

If your right hand is your dominant one, then use your left hand to use the scroll wheel, because you need your dominant hand to almost conduct yourself, to move around in the air and to be physical with the script.

In a way you need to create your own kind of basic sign language. If you really are a signer at all, then adapt that, if you really need to, but of course it's only for your own benefit. Nobody can see you. I've used this technique for so many years, and particularly when I have a difficult sentence, usually a long one where I can't take any breath, by moving my hand in a circular horizontal motion just makes the job much easier, as in the hard sentences, or when tired, I turn from a human into a voice machine with the wheel turning and the voice coming out of the mouth automatically!

If there is a multi-syllable word that I find hard to crack, like conceptualization, or evapotranspiration, you can split these words into individual syllables, but they still don't often become easy to actually say at normal speed. But "conduct" yourself with a moving finger and amazingly, these words become easier to pronounce at speed. Some medical experts will say that this is really just distracting your mind- which is so hung up on doing the word properly - by doing something else, and that may be true, but all I know is that this system works for me, so please try it out!

And it does work, because if you are forced not to move your limbs at all, voice over work becomes extremely difficult. Try it! It's awful! So if you aren't using your dominant hand to conduct yourself behind the microphone, you are making life very hard for yourself. It improves everybody's performance to be physical with what they are saying, as long as you don't hit the desk or microphone stand - it's a great tip! Being physical really helps with character voices as well. Maybe one character swaggers around a bit when talking, so you can do this while keeping "on mike" or another always feels pain, so you could grasp one wrist hard with the other hand when you're doing these lines. Remember, nobody can see you and being "physical" can really help a voice performance.

27 - THE AUDIOBOOK EDITING PROCESS

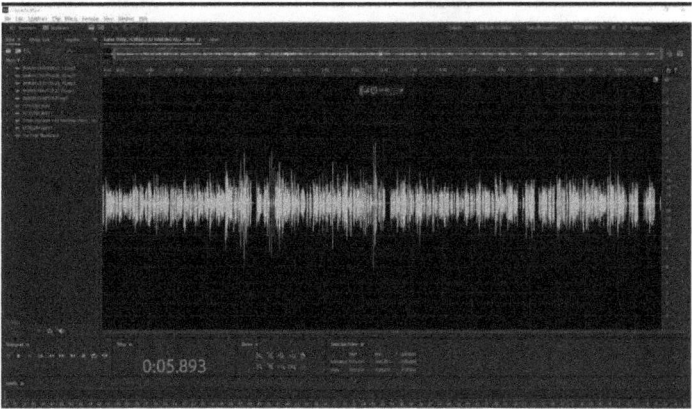

Everyone has different ideas about when to do the editing of audiobooks. In my own opinion, and I have tried all the different ways of doing it, it's far better to record a couple of hours' worth of recording, in 20 minutes sections in the morning, and then have a completely new session for doing the editing of that's morning's recordings in the afternoon or evening.

We have experimented with doing editing as we went along, in other words reading about 20 minutes' worth of narration, and then editing what we had just done , before going into record again. But I think there are two completely different mindsets you think differently when you're a narrator and when you're an editor. And if for example you are more of a narrator than an editor or more of an editor than a narrator, there's bound to be one type of work way or not that confident, so it's best really to separate the two tasks to different times, and even different computers and locations. You may have a great "listening area" at home, where you can play back and edit on big HiFi speakers and that's another advantage of waiting until later in a dedicated editing session.

So how do you edit audio files? Well you do it using the same software that you've used to record, and there are so many choices of software out there, but if you want to be seen as a professional, and to have the ability to make lots of little changes and tweaks to your work, then I would suggest you subscribe to Adobe, and download Adobe Audition - one of the creative cloud software programs.

Many people will say that for audio books, this is a sledgehammer to crack a nut, because Adobe Audition has got so many different features, some highly complicated things that you would never need even as a working voice over, let alone for the fairly technically simple work of putting together narrations for audio books.

That is all very true, indeed Adobe Audition has got so many features aimed at musicians, and music producers, and not just voice overs. And when will you ever need to use the multi-track facilities, when most audio book producers don't want you to add music or sound effects, or to process the sound to add reverberation, or to make your voice sound artificial, and so on.

But the thing is, one day, you may want to expand your offering in the world of voice over and audio production even more, and that's where a software program like Adobe Audition would be excellent for you.

If you know that you're only going to do audio books and nothing else, then a technically simpler program would do the job for you absolutely fine. If you think you're going to expand your portfolio in future months or years, then start with learning Adobe Audition, it is the Rolls Royce of audio software, it is the industry standard, you'll impress audiobook and video game producers when you say you have it, and in fact please check that out if you'd like a really comprehensive training on how to use Adobe Audition in great detail.

So what are the choices if you don't want to pay for a subscription to Adobe Audition? There are loads of free and fairly inexpensive audio recorders and editors out there, but I would highly recommend two. The first one was put together by a lot of volunteers using open source software, and it's called Audacity. It's available for Windows and Mac and it's got lots of great features that seemed to be added to quite regularly. It certainly won't have all the whistles and bells of Adobe Audition, but for simple recording and editing waveforms, and exporting as the types of files needed for audio book production it's absolutely fine, it is absolutely free at the time of recording. You can of course donate if you find the software useful.

The other program that we would recommend to you is also free for non-commercial use and it's made by Australian company NCH, and it's called Wavepad. We like this program a lot, and I think that's because it's very similar in the way of working in Audition, that I have been brought up on, but it's also got some features for voiceovers that even Audition hasn't got, for example file splitting. I've even put a video on YouTube about how to use this Wavepad program for file splitting where it senses silent gaps and then automatically creates individual files, in one click, which is so useful for when you're doing an E learning program or many phone prompts where you want to create individual files from one long recording.

All editing programs basically have a very similar interface with the waveform appearing on the screen and various controls to cut out bits add bits in or to change the sound of things, so let me show you how to do things in Adobe Audition, and I'm sure you'll be able to work things out for your own software program of choice. What we're going to show you is more of the tips and techniques to make your life easier, and not the actual buttons to push, which no doubt will be slightly different for every program.

After you've done your editing, you need to semi- master your files. In other wise exporting to mp3 and saving these in a folder, you'd call SEMI MASTERS. There's no point fully mastering yet, In other words getting all the files specifications ready for final delivery, because no doubt the author or publisher will have changes for you to make. And these changes you'll do on your original "full fat" WAV files. Yes, you WILL be exporting your big wav files here as the much smaller .mp3 files to send to the author as they are quicker and easier to send.

The mp3 files will still be far too big to attach of course, you need to upload your semi-mastered files to a file sharing site like WeTransfer.com, get the link and paste that into an email to your author or publisher. Then they can download the files at their end, and get ready to listen through with a pen and pad to hand to make their requested changes, which of course you hope are minimal! So how do you deal with the feedback notes from the author?

That's what we'll be doing in the next section.

28 - EFFICIENTLY DEALING WITH THE CLIENT'S NOTES & CHANGES

Once you have completed the recording of your often-huge manuscript, and at last you've scrolled to the end, it's also a huge relief as well! Most narrators tend to send files chapter -by-chapter as they are completed to the author, but some authors prefer you to send everything at the very end, it depends how busy they are. But one thing is for certain, after some days or weeks, you're going to get some revisions to record! Your heart may sink at pages and pages of little changes that have to be made, but quite often they look worse than they actually are.

But your life can be made much easier if you can communicate with your client beforehand how you want those notes and revisions sent to you. If they simply resend the script with highlighted bits that they want redone, with notes in the column, it's going to be very hard for you to be able to find out where in the actual audio file is the error or revision.

You may also get this scenario – you could have an author who, on hearing your recordings, change their mind over a section and send you a re-written script for that part! If there are a just a few of these, you would probably not complain, but I know of a fellow voice actor who was sent a completely revised Word file of the whole audiobook with many changes throughout, but the author hadn't marked down EXCACTLY where the changes were made. You would have thought that the author would have at least highlighted the new sections or given the page numbers and "in" and "out" words where the new bits were. So there was no way round it but to record the whole 7 hour audiobook again! In that case, the author did pay a little more when they eventually understood how we narrators work, but it shows how important it is to have a good technical relationship to begin with, before you start recording.

So what I've done is to put together a message to send to the client to explain how I want feedback notes, but is written in such a way to show that it will benefit the both of us.

You basically need them to give you the time codes as well as the details of the changes to be made. These changes need to be listed in the order in which they appear, and the time codes are simply the time into each chapter. No matter what system they are playing the file on, it will have a counter in minutes and seconds, for example the list could look like this:

Chapter 1

2'17" Sorry I missed spelled the Doctor's name here, it should be Smythe and not Smith.

15'03 Can you please re-record the whole sentence "Alongside the stream – to – "…allowing herself to cry" It just needs to be a bit more poignant and not matter of fact; thank you.

19'22" Please leave another second gap/pause after the sentence ending "…in San Fransisco. "

22'20" – Just retake the section where Andy gets angry from "I can't believe" to when he walks away. He really has lost it by now, give it more emotion please.

And so on.

Clients who give you notes like this they are much easier to work on, because you simply go to your editing program and load up the appropriate chapter, and it's easy to find the words you need to re-record by zapping to the right time code in Adobe Audition or your own editing software, and off you go.

A quick tip is that if you have a list of time codes in one audio file, as soon as you start working on the early ones in the list, the later time codes in the author's revision list may then not be that accurate, especially if you have been asked to take things out or put things in, or you have been asked to speak slower or faster in earlier sections. This will snooker the timings in the list for subsequent edits.

So don't think that the author has given you wrong time codes as you continue, it's just that as you add or take material away, those later timings are going to be off. So that's why you need the manuscript document open as well, and to find the part of the file that you are in, simply identify some unusual words that wouldn't be anywhere else in the book, and put them into "find" In Word, and that's where you will identify the correct part of the manuscript which needs the work on.

29 - HOW TO MAKE EDIT REVISIONS ON YOUR FILES

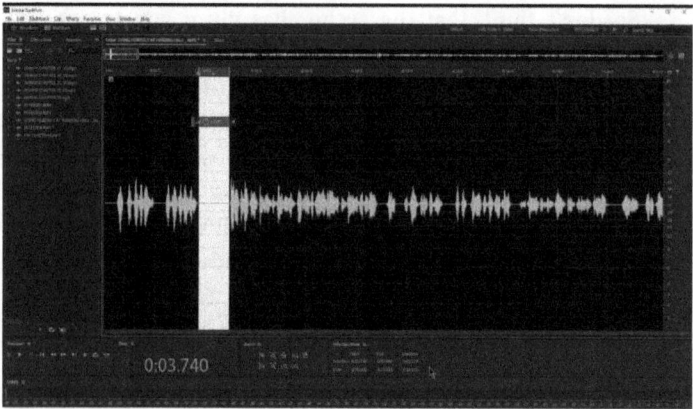

First of all and very importantly, you do not - I repeat do not - edit the MP3 files that you would have sent to your client. You go back to your original, uncompressed, larger master files that would be in a 24 bit .wav or .aiff format. Once you have made your changes to every chapter, then you would recompress, and re-export as an MP3. It is possible of course to make changes to MP3 files, but the quality will not be that good, and what about if there were further changes? You'd be doing further changes to another generation of an already highly compressed file where they can be nasty artefacts to your voice or background hiss increased. So always do editing on the original larger .wav or .aiff files, not on the smaller .mp3 files.

Be very careful that when you do rerecord, you listen back to the section before the mistake. Read along carefully to your own voice so you get the same kind of tone and speed and energy. Now open up a new file, and record the section that needs to be edited in. Highlight the new section and put it into memory; so it would usually be control or command plus the key C. Go back to the original recording and paste the new section in, and tidy it up. Now go back a good 10 seconds and play to ensure that it isn't obvious that you have rerecorded something and pasted it in.

Once you have sent the revised MP3 files to the author or publisher, there may be a few other notes before the whole thing is finished, but let's assume that everything is absolutely fine. So now you've got to so-call "master" the files, go through them all and make sure they are technically perfect so they don't get rejected by ACX or whoever is actually distributing the audio book files to the world. We'll be doing that in the next section "mastering and exporting".

30 - MASTERING AND EXPORTING AUDIOBOOKS

All audiobook producers worth their salt have strict technical parameters, so make sure you stick to these unless you want your work rejected! For example, with ACX or Amazon or Audible projects, they have many very strict technical rules and your files will be rejected if you don't adhere to them. But they are not being nasty just for the sake of it, actually they are on our side as human narrators, because they reject audio books that are created by computer and A.I.! Hurrah! Generally, if you get it right for ACX specifications, then almost certainly your files will be accepted by other publishers around the world. So let's take a look at all their rules and how we can practically sort them out.

To help with the encoding process with their system, and also to psychologically let the listener know they are at the beginning or end of a chapter, you must have 0.5 seconds of what they call "room tone", but is effectively "silence" at the head of every file, and 1 to 5 seconds at the end.

Now what about the levels? When you sent the files to the author, as long as they could hear them clearly, they're not going to care about technical things like levels, but they will care a lot when your files are rejected because the levels are wrong.

You must normalize to -3dB...not the full 100% you may normalize too usually, as it gives Amazon's dubbing system some headroom. Measure between -23dB and -18dB RMS and have -3dB peak values and a maximum -60dB noise floor. Put simply, all files must fall within a specific volume range. By keeping all files within this range - not too loud and not too soft - listeners won't have to constantly adjust the volume of their playback device.

So what sort of files do they want each chapter exported in? They don't want the big WAV files – no - they want MP3's but they have to be a certain type. No matter what kind of software you have, when you export, there will be a dialogue box where you can choose the exact specifications that ACX want for mastered audiobook files. The files have to be at a data rate of 192kbps or higher MP3, Constant Bit Rate (CBR) at 44.1 kHz. Before going on sale, titles are encoded in a variety of formats that customers have the option of downloading. So 192kbps (or higher), Constant Bit Rate MP3 files are required so this encoding process works without error. You may upload 256kbps or 320kbps files if you'd like, but the difference in quality heard by listeners will be negligible and they make for bigger files for no real gain.

So, do you export them and just send them off? Well, not quite, let's have a look at the other specifications that could get your files rejected, and a lot of them are down to your initial setup of your studio and your recording environment. Let's take a look at this right now.

ACX say that our submitted audiobooks must be consistent in overall sound and formatting. They say "Consistency in audio levels, tone, noise level, spacing, and pronunciation gives the listener an enjoyable experience. Drastic changes can be jarring to the listener and are not reflective of a professional production. "

Now the way to do that is if you follow our advice do everything at the same time every day, and also do it with the same microphone in the same recording facility as well you just need to get into the zone everyday so that you get consistency in the whole recording situation.

As well as providing all the chapters you do also need to provide separate files for the credits both the opening credits and the closing credits and there are certain things that you have to say. You can download from us the actual script that you can adapt to your own needs. At minimum, the opening credits must note the name of the audiobook, the name of the author(s), and the name of the narrator(s). Closing credits must, at minimum, state "the end".

As well as the credit files, you do also need to create an "audio sample" or sometimes called the "commercial sample". This is the file that you hear when you click on the "listen" button on the Amazon website. It needs to be between one and five minutes long, and it should start with narration, not any opening credits or music. It's basically going to offer customers a preview of the audio book, and it's not up to the narrator to choose it, it's best for the author to choose the selection that should be the "commercial sample". The author will know to select an intriguing part from their factual book, or in a fiction book, something that shows the flavor of the story, but doesn't actually give away any of the plot or spoilers.

Just to make it clear, you need to provide:

The OPENING CREDITS file

The CLOSING CREDITS file

ALL THE SEPARATE CHAPTERS, in separate files, all numbered and named correctly

And THE COMMERCIAL SAMPLE – the file that people can hear on the Amazon and Audible website when they're interested in buying the audiobook.

Back to the technical specifications - ACX and most other audio book producers insist on having either mono or stereo files but really would strongly suggest you use mono files , simply because they are smaller and there is less probability of them creating errors when it comes to phase issues or encoding. So make sure everything is just in good old Mono.

Each file that you upload as well as being in mono and being in the technical specifications that we've talked about, should never be longer than 120 minutes.

This is because of the technical system that's used for uploading and downloading. If the author has given you a huge long chapter that actually turned out longer than 120 minutes, you will have to split it into 2 or three, and a secondary section header must be included on continuations.

So if a section began with a header such as the narrator saying "Chapter 2", then basically you need to say "Chapter 2, continued" - and this will help listeners to easily navigate from one section to another. Talking of headers, in other words what you say at the beginning of a chapter, you must be absolutely consistent in this. So, for example, if you always say "Chapter One", without the name of the chapter as well, that's fine, as long as all the other chapters have just "Chapter 2", "Chapter 3", etcetera and not suddenly "Chapter 4 - The Chase Continues", or anything like that! All the headers the narrator says have to be consistent.

32 - GETTING WORK IN AUDIO BOOKS

So where can you find voice acting work in audiobooks? Let's talk about ACX, Amazon's Creation Exchange. Register on there and audition for a very wide variety of books of all types. So, check out acx.com. Once you have registered, you'll see via the top-right SEARCH menu the list of various scripts that are open for recording. It'll say "Titles available for audition". Then you'll see a screen like this. Some offer a payment per completed hour of audio – sometimes referred to as P.F.H. or Per Finished Hour, and you are bought out completely, you don't get another penny even if the audiobook sells millions; and some are 50/50 deals where you record for free – no payment at all - but receive monthly royalties. Our tip is to only go this royalty route if you have researched the author and it's already a book that is selling well on Amazon or Kindle! This is so important to do; you don't want to waste your time recording and editing an audiobook that won't sell when you've selected the royalty payment. You'll find many authors who already have an Amazon book, physical and/or Kindle, who are now looking for an audiobook version to sell as well. So simply take a few seconds to look up some of the reviews of the original book. If it looks hot, then go for it!

So if you decide to do an audition for a fiction or non-fiction book that takes your fancy, do the best you possibly can of course, unfortunately you can't hear anybody else's audition, but only take the time to make a demo for the author, if you're really sure you've got a good chance of getting it. If it's a subject you're not really into, or a type of book that you don't think you'll enjoy reading if you were a consumer, why put yourself through misery?

There should be plenty of other books out there, available for audition that will be right up your street, that you'll enjoy, and what's more, and more importantly, the listener will hear that you are really into the subject as well, so audition for these instead.

Normally the audition script is about 10 to 15 minutes long. If it's a fiction book, normally there are sections of narration, and also some character work as well. Don't bother too much about getting the characters exactly right, because maybe the author hasn't really thought yet about what voices should be assigned to each of his or her characters, so don't message the author for these details before you start, they just want to hear your audition and your own personal take on what you think the character could sound like.

You would record and edit the file, put some light compression on, and then upload the MP3 file to ACX, with a short message that doesn't include your personal contact details, and then wait. It may be a few weeks or even months before you hear back, so don't be despondent, some audio book projects really are spread over a long time, it's not like TV or radio commercials which are often done on the day!

When you do get an offer of a job through ACX, you have to agree to work with the author or publisher via the ACX website, and give them some realistic time frame of when you are going to deliver the files. You'll get various agreements that you need to click on and the job starts.

I strongly suggest that you only do the first chapter before getting detailed feedback from the author. They may have loved your audition, but they may have changed their mind a little bit about the style of the narration, or of some of the character voices, so just record chapter one and upload it and ask for feedback , before proceeding with the rest of them. You really don't want to record the whole of the book again, do you?

At the end of the whole process, when all your files have been uploaded, including the commercial sample, the intro credits, the outro credits and so on, you then get paid via ACX, or the project goes into royalties, and you can look out for money paid into your account , usually by PayPal, every month.

As well as ACX, there are very many other audiobook companies around the world, who might be pleased to hear from you. As discussed in the "Getting paid" section, Findaway Voices and Author's Republic have similar systems and models like ACX so you can hunt for auditions on there or create a narrator's profile.

But don't forget direct working with authors or publishers. In fact, if there's a book you love, either fiction or factual, if you're sure there's no audio version available, contact the author or publisher, say you're a fan and offer your services. I've been successful quite a few times with this method! There are plenty of independent audio book producers, for example, one of the biggest is BeeAudio, where they take you through a training process of their recording and checking system before offering you projects. In the UK, there is StoryTec where you can join their community of narrators and producers.

Sometimes smaller audiobook companies are set up to just accept the raw recordings from you, completely unedited and their own teams edit. Usually these production companies pay pretty low rates, but they do have to edit your material, and do all the other work related to bringing out and marketing audiobooks, so it is often a fair deal in the end. It may be a good option for you, if all you want to do is sit and read without the task of editing and cleaning up the files afterwards.

You may of course be approached direct by an author who wants you to record their audiobook. They don't want to go via ACX, even though they may actually publish it on that platform after you have recorded it, or choose Findaway Voices, Author's Republic or whatever. There is no problem with that, however, you really have to trust the person you are going to be working for. The ACX organization will make sure that the money from royalties will get to you or if you are being paid per finished hour, you will get your money for that too. So, if you are not going through ACX, do not work any "royalties" system.

There is no way you will have the time or resources to find out the sales figures. So you'll ask to be paid "PFH" or Per Finished Hour of material. We strongly suggest that you have a "staged payments" system in place. Ideally you would have an agreement that you would electronically sign and send it to the client so they would agree & that as well so both of you have copies as PDF files. You can download a sample agreement in this course that you are welcome to change and adapt to your needs. It includes a section on "staged payments".

KATY: Staged payments basically means chopping up the total agreed amount so it's fair for both sides. You wouldn't want to work on an audiobook for weeks, send over the master files, then send in your full invoice, and then it not being paid, do you?

So where do you start? First of all, you need to determine the approximate finished duration of the audiobook. If we estimate that your reading speed is going to be 2.5 words per second, (although some reading speeds can be slower at 2.2 or 2.3 or faster up to 3 words per second) then if you have a word count of the total text, simply divide this number by 2.5 and then divide again by 60 and then again by 60 to get the total duration in hours.

So, for example, if the total number of words was 125,250, and you'd find this in Microsoft Word by clicking REVIEW in the tabs, and then WORD COUNT in the top ribbon, you would divide this total number of words by 2.5, and that would give you 50,100. Divide this by 60 to give you 83.5. And divide by 60 again to give you 13.9.

So, the total duration of 125,250 words will take 13.9 hours.

Of course, this is very approximate, and you may want to adjust this up or down depending on the style and speed of reading that is appropriate for the audiobook. (You'd find out your own personal "Words Per Second" amount, by taking a minute's worth of your audition read for that particular book, count the words you read in that minute by using the script, and highlighting the words you read in that minute and using the word count tool again)

So if you have agreed a rate of say, $300 per finished hour, including all rights, then the total fee would be $4,175. If that was one of my jobs, I would divide that into three payments of $1000, and a final payment of $1175. Once the agreement has been signed off on both sides, send your first invoice for $1000, which should be fully paid before you start to record anything properly.

I assume by now that you would have recorded your audition, and would have worked sufficiently on the text, asking questions to the author or publisher, so it's obvious you have got the job, and they will feel that you are professional enough and have done enough ground work, to receive your first quarter of the final fee.

So when do the other payments get made? If you divide the full fee into four, as I say, the first payment should be at the start of the job, the second payment when you are about halfway through, and I do suggest that you send chapter or section as it is completed to the client, to prove you are actually doing the work, and the third payment should be when you have completed everything.

Of course, the client needs to listen through and will ask you to re-take certain sections. Almost certainly, you will get the dreaded "notes". Once you have worked through all the revisions, then you can send your final invoice in.

33 - AUDIOBOOK FAQ'S

❧

DO I NEED A STUDIO ENGINEER OR PRODUCER?

Of course, for major book releases you would have at least a studio engineer and a producer as well behind the glass in the control room listening to your every word giving you feedback. That's fine in a situation like big budget blockbusters like Jim Dale or Stephen Fry narrating Harry Potter, and so on, but for little old us in our individual voice booths at home, that is a big luxury, and would get rid of all our profit from the job wouldn't it? So that is why audiobook narrators need to really hone to perfection skill of listening as they are reading. Yes, the "three head technique" we discussed. For voice-overs and narrators working on their own, this is an essential skill. You haven't got someone else to say "Hey, you slurred that the third word" or, "You mispronounced that name", or "Why did you go faster at the end?" You have to be your own critic, and you have two learn how to listen very carefully so if you make a mistake stop and correct it.

WHAT IF THE AUTHOR WANTS MUSIC OR SOUND EFFECTS ADDED?

An audiobook is just that it is the narrator reading the words as you would see in the text version of the work, although usually adapted a bit audio recording, when there are visuals printed in the book obviously can't be seen in an audio recording. So soon as you start adding a few effects on your voice when the characters are for example in a cave you need to add reverberation or echo effects, or you're asked to add a bit of music when the action is getting a bit exciting, or you put in some sound effects when those Stuka fighters dive-bombing you in the third chapter, or whatever, you don't have an audiobook any more do you? It's more like a radio play! That's all well and good if that's what the client wants, however it gives you much more work to do. You just had his music somewhere for the sake of it, certainly the rest crying out for some kind of music as well isn't it? Oh, and while we're at it, although characters who are the opposite sex from you, the narrator, let's get an actor or actress in to do those lines then?! So, can you see, the whole animal has changed. So, this is why the leading producer of audiobooks, ACX advise against adding music and sound effects. A quote from their guidance says: "Don't include **music** or sound **effects.** We strongly advise against using **music** and/or sound **effects** in your ACX production. Our listeners often find these more distracting than enhancing, and rights and clearances **can** get very tricky when it comes **to music.**"

So even if you have found some music from a non-copyright library, still may not be cleared for your audiobook. I have personally actually produced an audiobook with music in, but it was only because the author had also written and performed the music gave me permission to use it only in the credits and not in the main body of the audiobook, and ACX said it was fine!

34 - SETTING UP YOUR VOICE ACTOR
RECORDING FACILITY

If you're just starting out in the world of voice acting, and you want to record at home, which obviously is what we suggest here, because it gives you much more flexibility, and saves you enormous amounts of money in travel and in hiring external recording studios, then this is what you need to do. The reason this chapter is at the end of the course, is because we felt that most people taking it would already have some sort of recording facility, but we didn't want to leave you out if you haven't set up a home studio yet!

Basically, when people book you as a voice actor, they don't just book you was that if you have a home studio, they book you as a competent technical person as well. There's no point you giving a fantastic performance, if you send your client a nasty distorted recording, which is off Mike, or full of hiss, or there are noises in the background. In the nutshell:

1. Get rid of external noises
2. Get rid of audio reflections

They're not expecting you to be as professional and knowledgeable about audio recording as someone in a top city studio, but they have to be very confident when they book you that you are going to record your voice to a high standard and you understand the connections between you, if they are directing you and what to do if the line goes down. If you are not a technical person at all, and you feel that the worrying about the technical side of doing recordings or live direction, is going to affect your performance, then you will need to find someone who can help you, a technical buddy shall we say!

So where will you build your studio? You need to find somewhere in your home which you could turn into an audio recording facility. I won't be so grand to call it a "studio" as such, but it may well turn into such! There are two important acoustic factors here. One is that you need to be away from external noises, so ideally away from a busy kitchen, bathroom, any noisy plumbing, or traffic noise. And the second thing is you need to have a room which doesn't have hard surfaces in. You know when you speak in a bathroom, or you go to an Italian restaurant which has got hard floors and hardly any curtains, everything sounds echoed and nasty doesn't it? That's because the sound waves are being reflected all over the place. The microphone doesn't like this at all.

"The cocktail party effect"

Human beings have got this ability, called "the cocktail party effect", where you can work out what the other person is saying, even though there's lots of other noise in the background, like other people speaking. The brain is very clever, but the microphone isn't quite as clever as that. Yes, you can sort of rescue your noisy audio recordings - getting rid of background noise in software like Adobe Audition, but ideally, you want to initially record in somewhere that is very quiet, and also has been sound treated.

If you have got a bulging wallet, you may like to invest in a voice booth, which start at about $3000 and go up to about $10,000 or even $15,000, depending on the size and sophistication. Mine cost about $5,000 and it's small but does a great job. Sound booths are basically boxes that cut out a lot of sound and are acoustically treated inside so that the sound waves have minimal reflections, and so it sounds acoustically dead. Quite often, you will need to tune a new voice booth, depending on where you are going to be sitting or standing in it, and almost certainly install some bass traps in there, to get rid of any boxy sound, which particularly affect smaller voice booths.

If you clap your hands inside a professional sound booth it sounds like you're outside, there's nothing to reflect against. So what happens if you can't afford a voice booth? First of all, you need to find the quietest areas of your home. And particularly at the time of day when you're likely to do recording. Just stand, close your eyes, and listen very carefully to what you hear. Yes there's the central heating making noises, there's the refrigerator that comes on every few minutes, there's a cat meowing outside, and that guy with the leaf blower will be coming in an hour. It's amazing how many noises we don't actually hear, because we're so used to them, but a sensitive professional microphone will pick all these things up. So go round your home and identify some possible locations.

Well many people start off in their clothes cupboard, or closet. If you're surrounded by lots of clothes, these do a similar job as acoustic tiles, they absorb sound reflections, and you can set up a light and microphone in there and be quite happy recording, if you don't mind it being a bit stuffy.

Many beginner voiceovers start off in their closet, simply with a microphone and pop filter, a microphone stand, so you wouldn't be touching the microphone, and they'd read scripts off their tablet, phone, or a laptop that hasn't got a noisy internal fan, and then record on a solid state recorder connected to their microphone. Then after recording in their closet, they would take the solid-state recorder, connect it to their laptop, transfer the files and then edit their recordings. That's one way to start, but ideally you want to be able to record on a computer, which saves time, and also when you playback your files, you need pretty decent speakers, to make sure the sound quality is good. So let me show you now, what I would consider to be a decent audio recording setup, without breaking the bank.

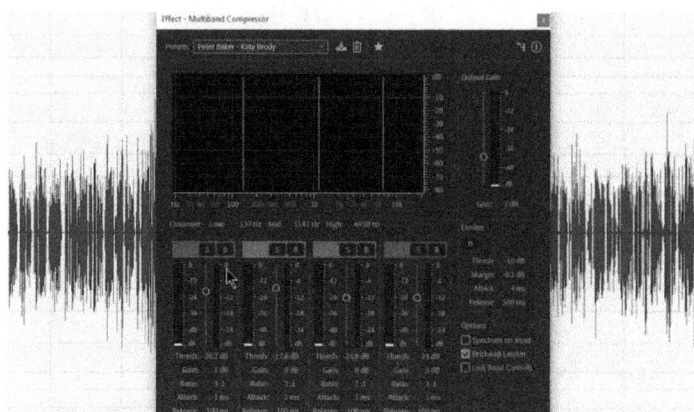

RESOURCES

This is a resource #1 for Voice Over Actor

NOTE: This document is intended to be a useful template for voice actors and audiobook narrators and is intended to be sent to the author or publisher of the book you are about to record and produce. You are welcome to adapt it in any way. The document is provided "as is", and we are not responsible for any misunderstandings or legal action taken if you misuse this communication.

Dear (Author's name)

As I'm sure you'll appreciate, any physical or Kindle book needs to be slightly adapted for audiobook recording, as an audiobook listener cannot see any visuals such as photos, graphics or speech marks. Do you wish to create an "audio-friendly" version, or will you let me adapt the manuscript for you with minor adjustments? For example, I will not usually narrate any references to photographs or illustrations; I will not narrate the index or the dedication page or any of the legal publishing information that is in the printed version of the book. Do you need "About the Author" recorded at the end?

I also notice that the chapters of your book have titles, but no chapter numbers, so I will assign chapter numbers to go with the chapter names to assist the ACX audiobook upload process and to help the user navigate the chapters. Is that OK?

Maybe you wish to go through the whole manuscript and slightly adjust certain scenes for audio use; if so please let me know, and advise when the fully checked audio version of the manuscript will be delivered ready for recording in my studio.

Could you please give me a few sentences about the main speaking characters in the book please? Let me know their approximate age, the type of person they are and any relationships they have with other characters? Let me know any style of voice or accent you have got in mind for any of the characters. You are welcome to send links for me to hear by other actors on YouTube etc., if it helps.

I would also need to know how to pronounce your character's names and also place names that are not obvious. Please could you kindly send an audio recording saying slowly these names? Many thanks.

(LIST OF ANY UNUSUAL NAMES)

Unless you tell me otherwise, I will record and edit and master the files to the standard ACX technical specifications. These are as follows:

There will be a standard Intro credit and Outro credit file supplied using the official ACX script:

Intro credit: This is (title of book) written by (author) narrated by (narrator).

Outro credit: This has been (Title) written by (Author) narrated by (Narrator) copyright (Year) by (Author / Publisher). Production copyright (year) by (author / publisher)

The technical standard of the files that I will provide, unless you specify anything different will be:

16 bit mp3 audio files 192Kb/sec; 44.1KHz sampling. Normalized to -3dB with light multiband compression. No music or sound effects.

Every file to start with half a second of silence, at the end of each file to end with 3 to 5 seconds of silence.

Please forward the full manuscript when it's finalised and I'll offer my best quote and an agreement about rights and exact delivery dates of the chapters.   However, if you commission me today, I can promise to deliver all recordings by (DATE) at the latest.

I look forward to working with you on this project.

Best wishes   (NARRATOR / AUTHOR)

This is a resource #2 for Voice Over Actor

NOTE: This document is intended to be a useful template for voice actors and audiobook narrators and is intended to be sent to the author or publisher of the book you are about to record and produce. You are welcome to adapt it in any way. The document is provided "as is", and we are not responsible for any misunderstandings or legal action taken if you misuse this communication.

Narrator Agreement and Contract

Between (Narrator / Producer)
And (Author / Publisher)
Project name:
Date:

1) (Narrator name) is a professional voiceover based and is independent, with no exclusive agent or representation of any kind. Contacts and payments shall be made directly with him. He/She is based in (Country) and is not / is at present registered for Value Added Tax (VAT).

2) (Narrator / Producer name) has sent a recording of a free, no-obligation sample of the project to you. This agreement and contract is for you to agree that you would like him to either:

    a) Continue to record the rest of the project in this style.

    b) Offer extra editorial and technical direction another sample page will be recorded. This second demo is still free. Third and subsequent sample pages will be charged at $ X US.

    If you are not happy with the sample selection, there is no obligation to continue and you can ignore this agreement and contract.

3) (Narrator) shall render performer's services in connection with this engagement in a cooperative and professional

manner to the best of a performer's ability, and subject to producer's direction and control.

4) The fee for the recording, editing, optimisation (using Adobe Audition) and the sending of the files to you is as follows:

(NUMBER OF WORDS) / 2.4 = (X)

X / 60 / 60 = Y = Amount of hours, the duration of whole audiobook.

Total cost = Y x (Hourly rate) = $Z

4 staged payments are asked for as follows, about a quarter at these stages:

PAYMENT 1 – START OF RECORDING: $Z / 4

PAYMENT 2 – MID POINT OF RECORDING : $Z / 4

PAYMENT 3 – END OF RECORDING: $Z / 4

PAYMENT 4 – AFTER COMPLETION OF RE-RECORDS : $Z / 4

5) Files shall be delivered by internet file transfer as either wav, aif or ACX compliant mp3 files. After 14 days, if the master files are required again, an extra fee of $X shall be required.

6) The fee for this project includes full "buy-out" with no future monies being requested or demanded in the future. The "buy out" includes selling on, downloading, duplicating on flash media, CD and DVD, as well as encoding in software, apps, devices and in public announcement machinery for perpetuity.

7) With the rights of the voiceover recording given over 100% to the client, (Narrator / Producer) shall not be held liable in any way for any legal action as a result of the content of the material being broadcast or distributed such as the script causing offence or breaching copyright in any way.

8) The client confirms that they do own the full legal rights over the text material (Narrator / Producer) has been asked to record.

9) (Narrator / Producer) agrees to complete the project in 3 working days, assuming he has the full and final script. Any re-takes due to errors in the script or in changing style by the client(s) will be charged for again at the normal rate.

Agreed by Author / Publisher
Signed:

Signed:
NARRATOR   /   **PRODUCER**

About Us

We hope you appreciate this resource to help you master the work of the Voice Over Actor. We offer a wide range of courses and books for acting beginners and professionals, voiceover artists, voice job marketing and also courses on presentation skills, confidence and also video filming and editing.

To learn more, visit: http://actor.academy